Currently the Chair of the Board for a not for profit based in Sydney, Australia, CJ Walmsley has three decades of experience in HR, change and management development working for seven multinationals and a long list of clients as a consultant.

CJ Walmsley holds a degree in business majoring in industrial relations and a masters of science in organisational psychology. CJ has worked in 17 countries and been based in six different cities – and never seen a statue built to committees.

To contact the author, visit her website www.cjwalmsley.com.

How to Be a Decent Boss

And Still Get Things Done

CJ Walmsley

How to Be a Decent Boss – And Still Get Things Done

EPUB format: 9781925579055
Print on Demand format: 9781925579062

Cover design by Red Tally Studios

Publishing services provided by Critical Mass
www.critmassconsulting.com

INTRODUCTION

You might not change the world. Few people do, but when you're a boss, when you're in charge of other people at their work, you have a tremendous influence on how they feel and consequently on how they behave. You change the daily existence of some individuals more than you think. Sometimes your influence goes beyond the time in their life that was spent reporting to you.

You might not like having that influence. You might not want to acknowledge that it's there, but denial is not helping you, and it's probably not doing the people who report to you any favors either.

Thoreau wrote that "the mass of men lead lives of quiet desperation." It doesn't have to be that way for your team, and even if it has become a bit desperate, the situation can still be turned around.

There are things that affect the morale of the people who report to you that are outside your control, such as the weather, badly behaved customers, and greater market forces. But how you behave toward employees, the example you set and the things you pay attention to, or ignore – these are entirely within your control.

This book is about trying to maintain your decency and sense of humor while still being an effective boss. The work has to be done, but this is a guide to reducing the risk of "quiet desperation" in your workplace. It's not aiming to turn you into a Super-boss or faultless guru on the mountain top because let's face it, that's not going to happen.

Leading versus Managing

The words "boss" and "manager" are used throughout this book. I think the word boss deserves a comeback. The word leadership has been beaten to death. Leading is certainly part of being a boss, but it's only one part. Looking to sports champions and five-star generals for leadership lessons has distracted too many ordinary workplace bosses from getting equipped with some of the basic skills required for influencing others, such as listening skills and self-control. The leadership industry has also resulted, rather unfortunately, in the neglect of the other critical elements of good management, such as planning, organizing and controlling.

Some current sentiments about leadership even go so far as to extol the leader at the expense of the manager. For example, "Managers light a fire under people, but leaders light a fire within people." Or, "Managers get people to do things, but leaders get people to *want* to do things." These statements all sound good on a fridge magnet, but they're not very helpful if you're managing the night shift at the supermarket and only half the casuals showed up and what you really need to do before dawn is ensure that the shelves are re-stocked. The driver of a concrete mixer does not need to be inspired by a leader with great passion who lights a fire. The driver of a concrete mixer needs to get in and out of a site safely and get the truck to exactly where it's needed to pour at the precise time. The driver and the shelf-filler report to human beings who represent the vast majority of bosses, managing people in very ordinary circumstances and making sure that the world we live in is functioning.

And plenty of managers are getting work done through others without carrying the title of leader. There are some excellent people running small businesses, charities, schools, hospitals, farms, and every kind of service or production team. Small businesses still make up the majority of employers. The boss may not necessarily wear a suit, attend meetings or call people into their office. Many won't have an office. They may not carry a business card. They may be called a foreman, lead hand, supervisor, team leader or coordinator. They might also be called Doctor, Guv, Sarge or just Boss, but they are all managers and the role they carry out is an important one.

How important? Everyone in our society has a stake in the way that management is carried out, and not just because supermarket shelves need to be refilled during the night and the concrete needs to be poured, although a world that is in working order is reason enough.

Management academic Henry Mintzberg wrote, "No job is more vital to our society than that of the manager. The manager determines whether our societal institutions will serve us well or whether they will squander our talents and resources."

The time, and therefore the lives and talents of people, can be wasted by bad management. Worse, employees can be driven to frustration and despair. Bad managers or terrible bosses can impact not only their employees, but potentially their families and their communities.

When you're first appointed to be the boss or manager, it's not easy to get advice about what you're supposed to do. Who guides you away from squandering resources? How do you know what success as a manager is, if your business rewards the wrong things? What happens if you have no mentor or helpful role model? Experience can be a very expensive way to learn. What would be deemed as common sense when it comes to dealing with the people who will report to you?

I've been working with these questions for more than thirty years in the kinds of businesses where people only wanted straight answers. For my own sake, and to get these people their answers, I've gone through more books and attended more courses and talks than I can recall. This is my conclusion: It's not easy to get clear, practical advice on the everyday concerns of a boss.

Too many management books are unhelpful and frankly, increasingly weird. I get palpitations reading titles that promise me power, vision, chaos, the chance to woo and wow, and above all, a sense of mastery. From the covers of some books it appears that managers can become warriors, sharks, psychopaths, monsters, wolves, winners, champions, and possessors of something called "First Rate Madness." Another title I've spotted suggests that a boss should avoid becoming an asshole. Are there people out in the world who knowingly choose otherwise? There are management lessons from Shakespeare, *Star Trek*, the dug-out, and even Genghis Khan. I sincerely hope I never work for someone who was inspired by reading the leadership lessons of Genghis Khan.

The genre is suffering for its self-centered focus on achieving power rather than learning how to use it wisely.

The fundamental need for decency and kindness in the workplace is barely mentioned. For many writers, leadership is only worth writing about when it's performed in large well-known organizations by overtly macho individuals.

I have two explanations for the problem with many management books. First, publishers are in a desperate struggle to compete and survive. Authors will invariably be told to come up with a title that really stands out or holds out a promise. Hence the endless titles about winners and champions and having it all NOW! But seriously, folks, organizing other people's work and getting results from a combined effort is a very old profession. There's a store of good sense around us, but common sense is not sexy and wisdom is not the word du jour.

Second, a problem lies in the unscientific nature of influence, and the inevitable disappointment that will follow our faith in any promises about human behavior. Dealing with people is not a hard science with correct answers and sure-fire models. Human beings don't come with an instruction manual. The titles may promise easy steps but that's a very misleading sales pitch. So is a short turnaround on competence. Ask any good manager if it's easy. Since when was any profession easy?

If finding the right book is a quest, then what about finding consulting expertise in this field? It turns out, that's not a problem.

An early piece of career advice I received was this: Never call yourself an expert, because an ex is a has-been and a spurt is a drip under pressure. We have gone way beyond the point of worrying about the word "expert." The lack of modesty in the self-promotion of leadership experts has become rather startling. I have been invited to connect on social media with people who have styled themselves as leadership gurus, "cultural transformation experts," founders of themselves, change agents and thought leaders, and yet I knew them fairly recently as mere mortals. It's very easy now to call yourself whatever you like and claim anything. So the problem of finding useful advice on managing ought to be easier, but in fact has become more difficult.

Would a series of five-minute talks equip you for the profession of management? This seems a laughable suggestion, but I have had clients ask if I could break down a leadership development program into short lunchtime talks so that the working day is not interrupted. It's as ridiculous as thinking that management skills can be developed online, but unfortunately, that's where the training of managers is heading.

Scott Adams, creator of the fabulous comic strip *Dilbert*, described another problem with many business books and experts. "I worked in a cubicle for seventeen years. Most business books are written by consultants and professors who haven't spent much time in a cubicle. That's like writing a first-hand account of the experience of the Donner party based on the fact that you've eaten beef jerky. Me, I've gnawed an ankle or two."

And while the publishing business faces the pressure to sell a product, the leadership speaker circuit has the challenge of putting bums on seats. Who wants to go to a really practical talk on being a good boss? Where will you find the ambitious speaker wanting to be quoted on how to sift a pile of resumes or give an employee some bad news?

I mean no disrespect, because people have all kinds of talents, but when I see invitations to talks on workplace leadership and the speaker is a retired politician, sports champion, mountaineer, academic or over-excited guru, I wonder – have they ever been tested by the day-to-day management of people? Have they patiently dealt with the (sometimes) trivial and infuriating issues of employees and customers while handling the outside world of inspectors, shareholders and suppliers that all provide a stream of challenges while the cash must continue to flow?

Even if the speaker is from a commercial enterprise, I still can't tell from a title on a business card whether they're a truly capable manager. I've sat in many audiences and workplace gatherings and listened to some very eloquent speakers who I knew for a fact were pretty dreadful bosses. *The Emperor's New Clothes* comes to mind. My first CEO was once the darling of the dinner circuit, a man the media talked about as a future political leader. Today journalists call him a corporate criminal, and they do this with impunity.

Large companies and well-known brands are not always helpful for finding good role models in leadership and management either. Too frequently, after being celebrated as "best places to work," they might have disappeared from view entirely, if they haven't exploded publicly and rather spectacularly. Employees inside those companies often tell a very different story to the PR releases.

Ultimately, the management of people and delivery of results is carried out in engine rooms, not in boardrooms. Rank does not guarantee cooperation. Respect cannot be demanded. I've seen many excellent managers at the supervisory level, and some truly appalling ones in senior roles who have screwed up on a monumental scale and then moved on swiftly in an upward direction. I've seen construction foremen managing large teams to meet impossible deadlines without injury and senior managers whose only "strategic vision" was keeping their eyes fixed on their bonuses and retirement funds. Before I listen to a person's pearls of wisdom, I like to seek out someone who has worked for them. Actions still speak louder than words.

And who am I to talk?

By this point you might well be asking, "Well, what are *your* credentials?" And that would be a very fair question. I'm not an established guru on management theory and I don't run a global organization, nor have I captained a rugby team, paddled a canoe down the Amazon or been forced to eat my own arm in a blizzard. Not yet anyway.

However, I have worked in the development and training of managers for more than thirty years. My career has taken me through very different businesses and different countries, through booms and busts, in companies that were the "flavor of the month" and some who were in big trouble. I've worked with managers at all levels and they have presented me with familiar worries, fears, gripes and problems. Watching the same issues come up over and over again makes me feel comfortable in writing about this subject.

My main references for writing his book have been the many hundreds of participants of management training programs I've run over thirty years. Thank you, everyone. I have been noting your concerns for a long time, and I hope I responded to them adequately when we met. I have also collected issues from in-house managers seeking support or advice on employee performance and from employees complaining about their bosses. It wasn't a terribly scientific method of research, but I kept a lot of notes on workable solutions. I've also made lots of mistakes. I'm quite happy to share some learning from the doozies.

I don't have ideas that will work for you every single time (and no one else does either), but I hope to share wisdom from some effective but fabulous nobodies. Only a small percentage of managers receive helpful training or support at the start when they need that help most of all. I believe this is getting worse, but in spite of this, extraordinary people often come through and make very competent bosses. I wanted to write about what these people do that makes us want to work for them.

I confess that this book also owes its existence to some of the people I worked with who got tired of hearing me complain about the state of management training today and suggested I do something about it or put a sock in it.

I have a particular motivation for writing this book, and it's not linked to any desire to be called a "thought leader." I'd rather be called an expert, and even that would make me break out in hives.

It's hard work being a manager if you're the kind of person who wants to get it right. Managers are under-appreciated maestros when things go right. They can become objects of ridicule when they get it wrong.

We work in a world where measures are deemed to be everything, but morale is hard to measure, and sabotage is even harder to gauge. Replacing morale with the word engagement doesn't change the problem, but for a long time I have believed that you can see morale if you know how to look for some of the unobtrusive measures.

For example, and these are just a few things to look for:

- Where do you see employees looking genuinely interested in their work?
- Which bosses have employees who are often sick or turning shades of grey, dragging themselves along almost visibly, counting down to home time?
- Who gets cooperation without raising their voice?

- Who gets sabotaged and doesn't even see how it is happening?
- Who bitches about their staff and complains that they can't take a proper holiday because all their employees are hopeless?
- Who tries to find opportunities for their people to move on in the world?
- Who is quick to take the credit for success, and similarly quick to blame an employee for any problem?
- Who has employees that tend to move on to better things because they're confident and equipped to do so?

Typical managers, in my experience, tend to worry about uncertainty, losing control, and the behavior of the people they have to deal with. They can feel real loneliness and frustration. They usually want to make timely, sensible decisions and handle people issues with confidence. They fear complete disasters and want to avoid being described as one. Lousy managers are often oblivious to the fact that they are an object of derision, and if informed of this, will shrug it off pretty quickly or turn it into a virtue.

I know that it's the "people" stuff rather than the straight technical side of the work that gives the most angst. It's the grey areas that often have bosses feeling powerless or unsure whether anything can be done at all. What am I talking about? Here's a small sample:

- How do you tell the team about a new instruction or change that has already been decided upon and sound as if you support it, when you think it's a really stupid idea?
- What do you say to the employee with chronic body odor? Now the customers are complaining too.

- What do you say to the employee who thinks she's a star, when in fact she's got a lot to learn? Are you allowed to say "you're just not as good as you think you are?"
- How do you handle the fact that you are now managing the same people who you used to have beers and laugh with about the "boss"?
- What do you do about a worker who keeps breaking a new piece of equipment because he wants to use the old machinery? He shrugs and says "It's useless! It keeps breaking down. Better go back to the old one." What is going on?
- What do you say to an employee who is technically brilliant, but cannot possibly be promoted because of his behavior toward people?
- How can you influence morale when you're feeling completely demoralized?
- What do you say to an employee who keeps wearing inappropriate and revealing clothing to work, when you don't want to end up being accused of being sexist or start up some social media war with the easily offended?
- What are you supposed to do, if anything, with workers who cannot stand each other?
- How do you try to appear normal, when you know that everyone is going to be out of a job within the next six months?

*

The first part of this book covers the role of any boss: the basics, the realities, what you absolutely need to do, and what you don't. The second part of the book focuses on the people issues, like finding good people, keeping them, and if necessary, letting them go. Throughout I have attempted to address the kinds of issues that I've listed above and talk to the bosses who take these kinds of worries home.

There are certainly some bad bosses out there but there are great ones too. Journalist Charles Kuralt wrote that "the everyday kindness of the back roads more than makes up for the acts of greed in the headlines." This is a book for all the bosses working quietly and trying to get it right on the everyday back roads.

I believe it is entirely possible to be a good boss and a decent human being, and get home in time to have a life. If this sounds appealing to you, then you're exactly the sort of person I wrote this book for.

CHAPTER ONE

THE BASICS

HOW DID YOU GET THE JOB?
WHAT CHANGES WHEN YOU BECOME A MANAGER?
WHO ARE YOU RESPONSIBLE TO?
WHAT ARE YOU SUPPOSED TO DO WITH YOUR TIME?
WHAT ARE YOUR BIGGEST PRIORITIES WHEN YOU START?
WHAT ARE THE THINGS THAT YOU DO NOT NEED TO DO?
WHAT ARE THE TEN COMMON MISTAKES THAT NEW MANAGERS MAKE?

*

HOW DID YOU GET THE JOB?

A colleague sent this email:

I am coming to the conclusion that my boss is an idiot. Common sense is taking too long to emerge and I fear this idiocy pervading the entire senior leadership team. There is a terrible lack of communication and everyone spends their time jumping when the guy at the top jerks their string. It's interesting how the culture of an organization is so influenced by one person. He thinks that a conference once every couple of years and a few town hall gatherings each year, coupled with largely meaningless edicts that percolate down the organization, will cover the communication angle. It also seems that people who challenge him are swiftly dealt with and not spoken of again except where we know the microphones won't reach. The feeling of disengagement is very strong. There is a lack of contact between the bridge and the engine room.

My correspondent is one of the steadiest managers I've ever worked with. He's not a whiner and he's not paranoid. Today he heads a department of about seventy people in a well-known company. His employees tend to stick with him. He knows how to manage other people and large projects very well, but right now he's in a kind of hell. Every day his energy is being drained, unnecessarily. His loyalty and commitment are being chipped away. His manager may not be a malicious man; he may not even know that his behavior is generating such despair, but this situation is not unusual. The questions "How did he get the job?" and "Don't they (management above him) know what's going on?" will be uttered when my colleague and his peers congregate in any location – from the water cooler to the pub.

We've all seen some totally dishonest, arrogant, ignorant individuals stepping into management roles with supreme confidence, while the more modest and capable types of people miss out on promotion. Lousy managers can create despair, waste, disturbance and loss. They can even cause injury and fatalities at the critical end of the spectrum, through indifference or from having priorities that do not include human safety.

Good managers can inspire us and shape our lives in very positive ways. Our bosses may even become friends and mentors for life. They can promote innovation and opportunity, set us up for financial security and give us the opportunity to grow.

*

It doesn't have to be as bad as my friend's email, but his current working life of "quiet desperation" raises a question that every boss should ask of themselves: How did you get the job? Did someone tell you that they thought you had the right qualities to manage other people? And when you became a boss, did you stop and think about how you wanted to perform this role? Did you aspire to be an effective and decent manager of people, or did you just think it was a timely reward?

Being promoted to manager for the first time can provide a real sense of having arrived. You might have felt proud to have been promoted, or you might have felt as if you'd been dropped in at the deep end. Both thoughts may have co-existed.

Promotion may have come late in the day, long after you expected some increased responsibility. There could have been some feeling of sadness or guilt if the role became vacant through someone else's misfortune or fall from grace.

If it's your own business, then it probably seemed natural that you would be the manager of people, at least in the beginning. Perhaps you inherited the role of manager. However, if you're working for other people, promotion is not a given and the realities of the role can be something of a shock.

A couple of hours after she'd been told she was now the boss, a former colleague, Barbara, said she went cold and thought, *Am I supposed to keep everyone busy from now on? How on earth do I do that?* Another colleague, Tim, said he realized he was a boss when an employee nervously explained the inappropriate behavior of another employee to him. "When she paused at the end of her statement I thought, *why is she telling me this? Am I supposed to sort this out?* Somehow I'd assumed they would just bring me technical problems and I would just give technical answers all day. What was I supposed to do about something like this?"

Not everyone wants to be a manager; not everyone likes it and certainly not everyone is suited to the role. You don't have to accept an offered promotion into management. Others before you have turned the offer down and lived to tell the tale.

Sometimes an individual does not want to leave their trade. They love what they do and that's all they want to do. This is a perfectly rational and respectable choice. But if you accept the role, then get comfortable with the word "manager" and don't be embarrassed that you now have that title. We need people to manage and to get things done through others. We need people to make decisions, act and take responsibility in our workplaces and in our communities.

However you got the job of boss, even if it came about through corporate dart throwing, you still have a choice in front of you. You can join the membership of the You're Confusing Me for Someone Who Cares Club, or you can aim to give it your best shot.

The people who now report to you are hoping to be managed by a competent and reasonable person. It's likely that whoever handed you the responsibility was also hoping you understood the level of professionalism required. Henry Mintzberg, as mentioned in the Introduction, is amongst those hoping that you don't squander society's talents or resources.

WHAT CHANGES WHEN YOU BECOME A MANAGER?

One day, all you're required to worry about is the task you've been asked to do. If the person next to you is slacking off or messing up, it might irritate you, it might even impact you in some way, but ultimately it's not your responsibility. You are paid to get your own tasks completed.

When you become the boss, the total effort of the team is your responsibility. Someone who is slacking off or messing up on your team *is* your problem. When the people who work for you are bitching about management over a beer, that's you they're talking about. When someone gripes that they wish management would do something about a problem, they mean you.

In some companies you might get some guidance, coaching or training to get you started. You might talk to someone you regard as a mentor. But in the imperfect world that we live in, you may have to figure it out on your own.

Along with fears about respect, acceptance, jealousy and possible resistance, there are some common and pressing questions, such as: What am I expected to do and how am I supposed to behave now?

Mary Parker Follett, one of the first management consultants, defined management as the "art of getting things done through other people."

When you're promoted to manager you're paid to make sure that the work is done through the efforts of people reporting to you. So you need to start doing less of the task itself, and instead have a plan to make sure that others are doing it to the standard required. That's not all you'll be doing, but you need to start letting go of the habit of spending your entire day on the task. You were not made a manager so that you would perform a few management duties in your spare time.

At the first few levels of management or supervision you may be doing part of the task as well, particularly when a rush is on, or to show someone else what to do. But if you are promoted many times in your working life, you may find one day that you barely touch the task you're skilled in at all, and that a hundred percent of your time is spent managing.

In fact, at the very top of large organizations, employees are often surprised at the chief's original occupation. It can be many years since the most senior managers performed their original skill and they may have a trade or profession that's not even used in that organization. They have become professional managers.

If you have people reporting to you directly, even if that's one person, then you have become a manager and you are now part of the management structure. It doesn't matter what it's called at your place – team coordinator, process owner, foreman or supervisor – you're a manager. If you're running a very small business, you're a manager. Even if you prefer to think of yourself as everyone's best buddy, you're a manager.

It will help you enormously if you face this reality. Accept it and decide whether or not to do it well, or step aside and let someone else take the role. But don't step aside unofficially so that another employee is forced to take over the responsibility.

There's no need to dodge the title of manager. The subject of management suffers more than most for being overcomplicated by theory and jargon, but the word manager doesn't need to change. It springs from the Latin words "manus", meaning hand, and "agere", meaning "to act". So in the strict sense, being a manager means handling things. It carries the strong implication of action.

Is your behavior supposed to change? The short answer is yes, but you're not being asked to lord it over anyone, or go to the other problematic extreme and become everyone's mate. You're expected to be a lot more professional. You were probably showing great professionalism in your behavior in the first place. It might have been one of the main reasons you were promoted, but one of the toughest things for many new supervisors, lead hands and team leaders to come to grips with, is that you are a member of a new profession now. Management is a largely misunderstood, mostly unregulated and often taken for granted profession – but it is a profession. So you're now required to behave with a sense of *professionalism.*

The key aspect of professionalism (for any profession) is the management of one's own behavior. Professionals are supposed to think before they speak and consider the demands of the role they're in. You now have to take into account whether you're acting in a manner consistent with the way you want others in your team to act because they will copy your example. Looking in a mirror and asking the hard questions can be a new and frightening experience, but it's absolutely crucial to get some insight into your own behavior if you genuinely want to be a good boss. And if you have poor self-control, then things are going to get ugly. Leonardo Da Vinci noticed this problem a very long time ago: "He who cannot establish dominion over himself will have no dominion over others."

WHO ARE YOU RESPONSIBLE TO?

In the language of business textbooks, managers might ask themselves when making decisions: Does this action increase the sustainable competitive advantage of our enterprise? But that's a bit unwieldy, so here are some other questions that break it down into digestible pieces.

- Who owns (or funds) this thing – and what do they want?
- Who do we provide a service or product to – and what do they want?
- Will this decision assist our business (or our part of it) to survive and prosper?
- What is the long-term impact of continuing to take this option?

You don't have to go through these kinds of tests for every single daily decision. A lot of our work becomes habitual, and the answers or reactions may be linked to well-honed processes. We might not even go to these questions for a decision, such as whether to replace the coffee machine, but you need a compass of some kind to guide the bigger decisions or tough choices and to keep your team on track.

If it's your own business, then consider that first question carefully when you make decisions. What do you really want? Be honest with yourself. It's very easy for owners, or the self-employed, to feel pressured into expansion or being taken over, for example, and realize that somewhere along the way the reason why the enterprise was started has been forgotten.

If you're employed by a private company then you know that someone wants to make money from the business. There may be one owner, a handful of investors, or thousands of shareholders, but investors want a return on their investment. They don't necessarily demand it in the short term, but they expect it one day, and they want a greater return for their money than a bank account would have given them. This is not unreasonable. You must plan to succeed in their eyes, or that money could soon be heading somewhere else.

And if you manage inside a large, publicly listed enterprise, then be aware that shareholders, in increasing numbers, are voicing their concerns about the way companies are run. This is because boards of directors and managers have, in some cases, behaved as if they're lords of personal fiefdoms. By law, boards are not free to do as they please. They are trustees of other people's hard-earned cash.

If your business or group is funded by the taxpayer or ratepayer at a local or state level, then it's still hoped that you will provide a good service and use resources wisely. Taxpayers have little choice about funding you, but they are increasingly able to make demands in others ways and hold you accountable. Decisions must be made around whether resources are being spent to add value in line with the payee's wishes. What level of service is wanted and needed?

If you're managing within a charity or a not-for-profit, then you must stay very close to what the group is trying to achieve and how you can best use donor resources to reach the desired goals. How much is actually going to the intended beneficiary?

Keep the investor (or owner, taxpayer, donor or citizen) close to your thoughts as you manage.

Managers have to spin plates to deliver on customer expectations and the need to add value at the same time. And that's just the focus of the first question.

There is another vital responsibility you now carry and that is toward the people who work in the business and those they come into contact with while doing their work.

Health and Safety is not a bolted-on distraction from achieving a result. The habit of "doing things right first time", and having employees who question all methods, produces workplaces in which people take care. And because they take care, employees habitually consider the decisions they are making. When it's genuinely embedded in the culture, a safe workplace is virtually always a successful enterprise.

Conversely, running unsafe workplaces is not good for any business. A negligent health and safety culture can wipe out your business pretty quickly. Customers will avoid you and investors may flee. In some businesses you will have difficulty winning projects if you are deemed to be too risky. Insurers will charge exorbitant premiums, as will any staff with bargaining power. There is more about your responsibilities coming up under What are your Biggest Priorities?

WHAT ARE YOU SUPPOSED TO DO WITH YOUR TIME?

Managers plan, lead, organize and control. It's easy to remember that as an acronym if you think of a stone hitting water – PLOC.

If anyone asks you what you've been doing all day, then ideally one or more of these four activities should be included in your answer. (Ideally you're not being asked this question very frequently by all the people who see you at work.)

You're paid to PLOC, and if you fail to PLOC then things will start to go awry very quickly. This applies to every unit, team, department, small business, large corporation or corner shop. So, what do these terms broadly mean to a manager?

PLANNING is all about answering the question: "Where are we going and how will we get there?"

There is an old adage: "Fail to plan and you plan to fail." Plans don't need to be aggressive, but they do need to address critical questions.

- What outcomes do you want to achieve? If you don't have an overall objective, how will you know you've succeeded?
- What actions are necessary to achieve your objective? Plans must direct the organizers or else the desired outcomes will be missed.
- What control measures will you need to set up? You should be able to gauge at any time whether the plan is working.

If the plan is clear and relevant then organizing, leading and controlling become so much simpler. If it's not working, then the other functions can help to refine the plan. The functions of management are totally interrelated.

Bosses communicate plans with those who are essential to make it work. If you take the time to explain to staff how their daily tasks fit into the plan, and perhaps how your plan fits into a bigger picture, then it's very likely you will begin to have more motivated employees because you've understood the human need for meaningful work.

The vast majority of people want to believe that what they're doing matters, and that what they do is important enough to be done right. You might think that a temp staying for a few days doesn't need to know about where the business is going, but I've seen temps asking that question because they're genuinely interested. I've also heard managers insisting that their long-term employees are not interested in this information. I beg to differ.

LEADING *is about influencing people to achieve the plan.*

There has been a fairly tedious and ongoing debate about the difference between leadership and management. I once went to an all-day seminar on this subject, and it was ten hours of my life I'll never get back. I don't know how arguing about this helps to get the milk delivered or hospitals cleaned.

However, I would suggest that leading is part of managing. All managers have to lead (and plan and organize and control) but not all leaders have to manage. As an extreme example, heads of state and ministers in government have people reporting to them who plan, organize and control. The leader takes ultimate responsibility and needs to know about the plan, organization and controls, they just don't have to do very much of it. They lead, but they do not manage.

So what is leadership? In our everyday workplaces, leadership is about persuading people to follow you. It's about gaining people's trust in the decisions you make so they will support you with their cooperation. That is an art and not a science, no matter how many graphs and quadrants get thrown at the subject. You'll need robust communication skills, and I've included an entire chapter on learning those skills, but it's hard to simply acquire integrity or the knack for obtaining trust. These qualities attach themselves to us when we are consistent, and our reputation for integrity can only be earned. Trust is usually hard won over time and is so easily lost.

Employees will often say that a good leader is *approachable*. But how do you know if you're approachable? Here are a few positive indicators.

- Do people tell you about ideas they've had to improve the work?
- Do you stop and look at people when they talk to you in everyday work situations?
- Do you listen to people in a way that encourages them to speak?
- Do you speak to people in a way that encourages them to listen?
- Do you treat people as though they have a valid opinion and assume they have a desire to get things right?

If your reaction to such prompts was "I haven't got time, but they could make an appointment if they want" or if you genuinely feel that "they've got nothing to contribute" then that's worrying. If serious problems arise that have been festering for some time and noticed by employees, then you may have an approachability problem. Silence is not a good sign in a workplace, unless it's a library.

Some bosses exhibit an instant and noticeable slump in posture when an employee approaches them. They can even sigh or give a bored eye flick, though they may not realize they're doing it. Others will keep looking at their emails or anywhere else, or even walk away when they're supposed to be listening.

The skill of listening will be explored later in this book, but getting honest feedback in this area alone is a useful thing to do. We might believe we are approachable but our body language and facial expressions can give the opposite impression.

Some managers build barriers that make physical access difficult. Large potted plants, locked doors, bunkers, unwieldy PA stations and frosted glass are some favorite techniques to clearly send a "do not disturb" message. I once worked with a manager who had an extra lockable door built in her office when she found that employees could "just walk in" from a side swing door. The nerve! She organized and paid for the building work herself.

Leadership is also about accepting responsibility. Managers who have failed to accept responsibility in workplaces have filled the business pages, and sometimes the front pages of our newspapers.

ORGANIZING is about making sure the people who report to you have what they need to get the job done.

When Mary Parker Follett said that management is "the art of getting things done through other people" she was really saying that good organizers are critical to good management. They get things done. It is possible for someone to exhibit all the traits of a good leader and completely fail to deliver on the plan. It is possible to have a well-crafted plan that never moves forward. Something is needed to make things happen and so managers must be organizers.

Organizing is an underrated skill. It's about having good systems that have been refined over time and having the right people to operate those systems. This is so much easier said than done.

When you visit parts of the world where services and goods are not well organized you are confronted with the fact that we often take this aspect of management for granted. The skills of the organized manager and their teams are critical for keeping our power, water and traffic flowing, trash collected, ATMs stocked with cash, and the markets full of edible food.

Organizers start with the plan, and then ask "what is needed to make this plan succeed?"

- Does everyone have all the bits and bobs they need, when they need them?
- Do people know exactly what they have to do?
- Are all the skills and resources present in the team to achieve the plan?

If you can orchestrate labor, cash, inventory, equipment, paper, signatures, fuel, tools, safety gear or ingredients, and keep the output coming and the customer satisfied, and do this day after day, then you have mastered the art of organizing. Or perhaps you have people on your team who are expert at organizing? (If so, then hang on to them!)

CONTROLLING *is about checking how you're doing against the plan.*

Controlling is how a business disciplines itself. Managers perform this role, because of course a business cannot actually discipline itself.

Controlling is about looking at *what is actually happening* and knowing whether you're on course with your plan. If you're off course then you must take action to correct. To know what is "actually happening" requires systems, checks or methods that show real outcomes, or to be as sure of them as possible. For example, if I plan to sell 200 cars per month, and this week I sold 5, then my control systems (in this case, the sales figures) will alert me to the fact that I have a problem. And then come the questions for a manager – what is the problem and what am I going to do about it?

To survive, a business must play a good offensive game of winning business. But it must also play a good defensive game, and that means constantly managing how resources are being used and correcting deviations or problems.

The product or service needs to be delivered as promised. This applies to an aircraft manufacturer or a corner coffee shop. Good controls enable you to make a promise to the customer and deliver on it, and that's essential for anyone wanting to stay in business.

*

These basic management functions are highly interrelated:

- Good controlling helps you minimize waste in all business inputs: time, energy, money, machinery, inventory, payments, work methods and practices. This assists with smarter organization of available resources.

- Good planners assist good organizers to have the right resources in the right place.
- Good organizers need good controllers to alert them to corrections in demands.
- Good leaders enable organizers and controllers to get things done – ideally – right the first time, by clearing any barriers in their way.

The reason to keep these plates spinning and be effective at planning, leading, organizing and controlling is so that you ultimately add value.

I know this term "adding value" has been thrown around a bit, but it's only about questioning what you're doing and asking if it's making the business stronger and (usually) more profitable in the long run, without damaging its worth and reputation.

Examples of adding value include:

- being effective in inventory control without compromising delivery.
- reducing the cost of waste.
- finding ways to utilize waste that earns income.
- organizing to sell more and increase revenue.
- creating a safer, healthier workplace that results in lower absenteeism and productivity increases.
- creating a safer workplace that decreases insurance premiums.
- finding new markets for your product.
- negotiating better terms with suppliers.
- improving the product or service to increase competitiveness.

Sometimes we interpret innovation as pure invention, but all of these improvements to the bottom line are innovative.

*

It was a peculiar trend of the 80s and 90s that we started viewing the breaking up of businesses as a kind of talent. Cutting and reducing is not adding value if it slowly destroys the value of the business. Saying "no" all day doesn't take a lot of skill either – a tired toddler can do that. Sizing up the contents and selling them off is not leadership – it's a glorified garage sale, and when quality, business development, competent human resources, safety and training are cut to the bone or just dropped from the leadership agenda, you know that value is not being added and the business is terminal.

Your role as a manager will be carried out in an imperfect world. Mistakes will be made, delays will occur, costs can rise, people will ring in sick and your supplier's truck might break down. Life does not run to a perfect plan, but a good plan is a compass to get everything back on track. Planning, leading, organizing and controlling now constitute the major part of your job description, even if you weren't handed one. When you plan out your time as a manager, you now have at least four headings on the page.

WHAT ARE YOUR BIGGEST PRIORITIES WHEN YOU START?

Now that you're a manager, boss, supervisor, "big cheese" or whatever they're calling you at your workplace, there are some things that you should be doing right now, off your own bat. Every industry and profession and trade is different, so this advice is general. But every manager has explicit responsibilities and you should establish what these are very quickly.

1. Understand the legal implications of your role.

In one temp job, a long time ago, I had lunch in the staff canteen during my first week. Back at my work station, my face began to turn green and I was sent to the staff nurse. She looked at me and said, "When will you people learn to stop eating from that disgusting staff canteen?" I was lucky. At least I came back the next day after a memorable trip home on the bus.

How could I have known that a well-known company that actually sold food (among many other things) was serving up expired ingredients to their own staff? Where was the nurse's duty of care in this, other than to berate me for not being aware of this terrible fact? What went through the minds of the kitchen staff as they put, for example, shellfish going bad into staff meals? What can be said about my need to hold down the job that I didn't even complain when my wages were docked for leaving early with food poisoning?

So much has changed for the better in the world of Health and Safety management but people are still killed and injured in workplace accidents every day. We tend to hear about the deaths, but the statistics on serious injuries are frightening. Then there are cuts, scrapes, bruises, burns, broken limbs, and longer term injuries – like deafness – that people suffer while they're making a living. And just like my consumption of high-risk ingredients, many of these go unreported.

Safety at work has gradually improved but this was not due to luck. When I started writing this book, I'd been working for a company that had seen two employees killed in one year. The Health and Safety team was frequently heard imploring people not to take shortcuts, to stop and think about what they were doing so that it could be done safely. One of the safety leaders was often heard to say that "accidents don't happen by accident," since the overwhelming majority of investigations showed a very human cause. A split second's poor judgment or negligence can mean that someone isn't going home.

As a manager you have very clear legal obligations to keep the people who work for you as safe as possible. These obligations include ensuring that you never instruct anyone to do something that's dangerous without equipping them with training and support. You are required to investigate minor injuries and near misses and learn from them. You're also obliged to protect those who come into contact with your business, product or service, such as customers, visitors and anyone wandering through or close to your place of work. The consequences for ignoring your health and safety responsibilities (which you've automatically acquired by becoming a boss) are getting tougher all the time.

A first-rate Health and Safety director I know insists that "it's usually about people taking care of people, looking out for obvious risks and just thinking a bit. Most accidents occur through little things – a slip here, a messy floor there, a lapse in concentration, or a moment of kidding yourself that you've done something hundreds of times and therefore you're immune from danger."

In every kind of workplace – even sitting at a desk – there is some risk, but a boss must do all that they reasonably can to ensure that people go home in one piece. You don't need to wade through the legislation on your own. If you don't have some guidance in your workplace, then contact the Health and Safety organization that covers your industry, city or state or country. They can get you started with straightforward advice.

What other legal obligations do you have besides health and safety?

- You are going to be signing papers (or giving approvals) and sometimes people will ask you to sign them in a hurry. What are your responsibilities and limits? Find out as soon as you can about the legal and financial dimensions of your role.
- You are going to be managing people. What are you obliged to do in terms of employment contracts, rights and basic work conditions for these people? Do you have a Code of Conduct you need to be familiar with?
- You're going to be providing advice, products or services to people, customers and employees. What are their rights?
- What could happen to you if something goes wrong with this business? Do you need some insurance coverage to protect yourself?
- Can someone on a government payroll shut you down? Why would they do that and how can you ensure it doesn't happen?
- What about the tax department? What obligations must you meet with them?

If you don't know your basic responsibilities then you are exposed. Ignorance is not an excuse under the law. Find out about your legal responsibilities and then take them seriously.

2. Find a mentor, or better still, a few mentors, and be willing to learn.

Oh, you don't have an MBA? Well that's OK because in some organizations MBAs are no longer regarded with a friendly eye. Qualifications, courses and seminars make up a part of management education, but there are other ways to keep developing without taking time away from work or having to find the money for formal training.

One excellent means of getting an education in management is to find a few good mentors. In other words, simply ask for advice from some decent managers who have been there before you. Most people enjoy being asked for their opinion and are usually very generous with their help. One colleague shared with me his belief that "if you show any sort of willingness to cultivate a mentor or coach, they seem to materialize to help foster you and do what they can to help."

There is also the possibility of joining a special interest group in your industry, business field or trade, a chamber of commerce or small business managers' group that can support members with practical advice.

Some newspapers have business and finance sections, and sometimes a regular management education column of some kind. There are management magazines that can have useful articles on the basics.

"Textbooks are not just for flower pressing," one of my exasperated business tutors once said to me. If you are interested in the more academic side of management and don't want to pay for new books then look at garage sales and secondhand shops. Management and business textbooks are very useful for jargon busting at the very least. Thanks to the internet and print-on-demand publishing, some classics can still be found and downloaded. Being able to google basic questions has made life easier.

It's a good idea to know what is happening to the economy in general, the markets that are related to your business, your employment markets, and the demand for your particular product or services.

At a more local level it is always useful to know what's happening to your customers. How are your competitors faring? Set yourself the ongoing challenge to keep up with the market your business is in and stay informed. Who is surviving and why? Who has failed and what lessons can be learned from them?

Aim to speak knowledgeably about what is happening in the business world around you or even in your own community or industry. If you plan to be a good manager, you'll want to help steer yourself and your business around the icebergs as well as the opportunities.

3. Manage your behavior.

There is a lot more on this subject throughout the book because self-control is an absolutely vital element in good management.

This is something you have to wear from now on – you are a role model to the people who report to you. Your behavior is being watched (and invariably copied) whether you like it or not. People will view your behavior as an acceptable standard.

And here are some home truths about professionalism and self-control:

- You are always responsible for what comes out of your mouth. Think before you speak.
- If you don't already do it now – learn to appear calm. If you have a temper that you occasionally struggle with, then at least learn the skill of apologizing. Better still – learn to control your temper. The world will be a better place. If you are inclined to panic then understand that it's hard for people to work around that behavior. Learn to manage it. Get some honest feedback and find a steady mentor.
- Say "I don't know" when you don't know and set a good example for everyone else to be open about what they do (and don't) understand. No one expects you to be an expert at everything; don't pretend that you are.
- Approachability has been covered, but it's an important quality and deserves a re-run. Learn to put people at ease so that they can be open with you about what's going on. If you make people feel defensive – and many bosses do that without realizing it – then it's going to be very difficult for you to build trust and be approachable. If people feel too anxious to talk to you they might only tell you what they think you want to hear, rather than what you need to hear. Try to always see the person who talks to you directly and gives honest feedback as a valuable ally rather than a threat.
- You have to become far more conscious of how you are communicating on the phone or in writing. Read your message out loud if you can and try to put yourself in the shoes of the receiver. Emails are great for sending factual information but they are also a very effective way of sparking offense and misunderstanding at high speed. Be concise and remove emotive words. Invite questions,

and top and tail your messages with good-mannered greetings. And if you sense (from a terse reaction) that your communication has been taken the wrong way, then pick up the phone or go and see the individual (if possible) and sort it out. Only copy in other people to emails when it is absolutely necessary or appropriate, and never write an email when you are angry. If you wish to vent, write it with an empty address or send it to yourself. Open that email again in 48 hours and ask yourself if you still want to send it. I guarantee the answer will be "no."

4. Get more comfortable with thinking and decision-making.

I worked near a manager who could not make decisions. Staff went to her colleagues for an answer on the simplest things. They just didn't have the time to waste and did not want to keep customers waiting. She was even known to sit on annual leave requests for months, and in the meantime, the employee would have taken their holiday and returned with a tan. She replied to everything with a stock phrase: "I'm going to need some time to process this issue." Emails were replied to on average three months later, if they were replied to at all. You can probably imagine the level of frustration and the frequency with which employees began to go around her and then ignore her completely. This was not managing, by any definition.

Managers are paid to think and decide and see that their decisions are acted upon. Consensus is great if you have time but it's not always possible, or indeed desirable. (See Chapter Eight.)

To make the best decision you need information. You can often get this by asking the right questions and having people on your team who can speak to you honestly about what's happening. Ideally, you'll encourage people around you to feel free to speak up and steer you away from mistakes.

Do ask the "dumb" questions. They're rarely as stupid as you might think, and the only truly dumb thing is holding back or going ahead without the necessary information.

Remain decisive even when you've made mistakes. That doesn't mean staying with a bad decision, but admit to it, and don't feel you have to keep backing it come what may. Things won't miraculously get better. Being decisive means making new decisions sooner rather than later. People are far less bothered by the manager who can say "I made a mistake" than they are with the manager who cannot accept that they were wrong and takes the group, lemming-fashion, over a cliff.

WHAT ARE THE THINGS YOU DO NOT NEED TO DO?

It's useful to know about the things you don't need to do, in order to save your time and your sanity.

1. You do not have to be right and perfect all the time.

You cannot possibly be right and perfect all the time. You will make mistakes. Don't fret about that, just learn from them. Try to find something in the mistake that has some value. Some great discoveries have come from mistakes or unintended consequences.

You don't need (and can't possibly have) a ready answer to every problem. Learn to say "I don't know but I'll find out."

Don't be afraid to say sorry if you get it wrong. You will occasionally put your foot in it. You will make some bad decisions. Learn to acknowledge those times. It creates a very healthy work atmosphere if people then feel able to be open and honest about their own mistakes and concerns.

There is a big difference between a good try and a really stupid mistake. Appreciate the early admission of a mistake because the habit of hiding them from an overreacting, punishing boss has potentially dire consequences.

You will never be good enough for the whiners, but the vast majority of people who work with you are going to be rational, reasonable people who can handle imperfection.

2. You do not need to speak in a convoluted managerial style.

In fact, the opposite is true. A good boss should simplify things for people. Speaking plainly and politely works best. Jargon just increases the chance of misunderstandings.

Your aim is to help people understand. People also appreciate straightforward news. Say it without the gloss or spin. People tend to react against insincerity.

3. You don't have to learn your predecessor's opinions about other people.

Make up your own mind about people if you can. Don't close your eyes and ears to someone else's experience but someone in the team might be looking at your arrival as an opportunity to make a fresh start. So let them do that.

4. You don't have to accept (or be indoctrinated into) the way things are done around here.

Question "this the way it's done." Ask, and encourage others to ask "why?"

Two of the niftiest questions up your sleeve are: Does it have to be done that way? Does it have to be done at all?

5. You don't have to change everything for the sake of it.

Diane, who is older and wiser now, confessed, "I remember how I completely rearranged an entire floor after a promotion, just because I thought I was supposed to. The staff all looked at me as if I was mad."

I once threw out a load of files, thinking they were only a symptom of my predecessor's obsession with paper. For the next year I lived with the fact that I had needed some of those records and there were no copies anywhere.

Take your time. Some things will be working and are right for the business. Some things might need to change. Don't feel you have to change everything at warp speed.

6. You don't need to try to win a popularity contest.

You are there to manage. Professionals do not make decisions in order to be popular. Consider a doctor always wanting to make patients happy – how would that impact on the advice they gave and their future worth as the right person to consult?

*7. You don't have to win an Oscar for best performance in a
dramatic role either.*

Jerry, a manager I have enormous respect for, explains this
point very well. "I have felt that some other managers, and
even some employees, have wanted me to shout and scream
to get things done, or to get angry about things that simply
don't make me angry. It's not in my nature to lose my temper or
talk over people. People need to be confident about their strong
suits and not try to manage in the image of someone else."

I once had to try and convince an employee to apply for
a supervisory position. The senior leaders in the business
wanted to hand the promotion to her, but they were obliged
to go through a formal process. Unfortunately, she flatly
refused to apply for the role, saying, "I just couldn't yell
at people the way you have to. I think I'd be too upset."
Having worked for a roaring dinosaur for years, this woman
assumed that his aggressive behavior was not only normal,
but a requirement for the role of manager.

*8. You don't need to know the tricks of motivating and
influencing people.*

I have written an entire chapter on the subject of keeping
people, but for now I'll just say that there are no guaranteed
tricks for motivating people.

WHAT ARE TEN COMMON MISTAKES NEW MANAGERS MAKE?

There are some common traps that newly promoted managers
walk into and I know I have been guilty of most of these.

I suspect any mentor or role model that you admire would own up to at least some of these, so you needn't feel alone if you recognize yourself here.

1. Denial (or hoping this will all go away).

I was part of a teleconference a few years ago when a man with the title of Regional Manager, who had over 200 people reporting to him, said "the problem is that management needs to talk to my staff about what's going on and listen to their concerns."

What is wrong with this picture?

Pretending that management is still "somewhere else" and "someone else" is common and it can settle in as a bad habit.

If you're not called a manager then you might not realize you're part of management. And you might not have wanted this change in your working life. With any change that we don't like we can go into denial or pretend it's not happening, but this denial will mean that the responsibilities of planning, leading, organizing and controlling will be neglected.

2. Trying to do everything.

There are a few reasons for the "headless chicken" problem in new managers.

One is to do with comfort and security. A voice in our head might say, "I know I was good at the task I had before and I felt sure about what I was doing. I'm not confident at managing, so I'll keep really busy with the old task because that makes me feel like a useful and capable person."

Another reason for trying to do everything is because we don't understand the new role. Managers are paid to get results through the actions of others. Commonly, new managers complain, "I'm so busy. I've got too much work to do now that I'm a manager. I don't have time to plan and lead and all that other stuff."

That's partly true. You do have work to do, but the new work is managing, not working all hours to the point of exhaustion.

It's understandable that you can feel so responsible you try to make sure the work is done perfectly or too quickly and you overdo it.

New managers can sometimes feel that they must keep earning the confidence of the person who promoted them, as if that trust is a fragile thing. This can manifest itself in trying to ensure nothing goes wrong, which can result in a lot of overtime for the new manager, and often some of the helpful but bewildered team members.

You have to let go of the task, or at least a very big chunk of it, so that you can plan, lead, organize and control. Trust the people around you as you were trusted.

3. Believing that you must be right and perfect all the time.

> Nothing would be done at all if one waited until one could do it so well that no one could find fault with it.
>
> Cardinal Newman

New managers can insist that things are done their way as if that's the only possible way to reach the result. They may also believe that they'll look bad if they're seen to be wrong or imperfect in any way. It's a nightmare in the making but most people get over it.

If this delusion settles in for a long run, it breeds a control-freak manager.

4. Believing you are superior to those you manage.

I asked a young manager why he wasn't getting out from behind his desk and just talking to the people who worked for him. They were commenting that he had barely spoken to them. At first I thought he might be shy, but it was worse than that – he had not even considered meeting the people in his team. "Why would I want to talk to them?" He shrugged and sneered as he said it with an unfortunate emphasis on *them*.

There are still, sadly, too many managers who genuinely believe they are above the people they manage. New managers can adopt this belief with frightening speed. The highly insecure new manager will frequently remind people of their importance, start ordering people around for the sake of it, use phrases like "my people," "my team" or "my boys and girls."

Use a label like "superior" often enough and you can delude yourself into believing that you are superior to the people that report to you. Employees can be similarly hypnotized into believing that they cannot speak to "them up there." This belief in the superiority of managers can develop because of the cringeworthy workplace terminology we still choose. There's no room in the modern workplace for words like superior, subordinate, or master, and phrases such as "the coalface," "those higher up" and "those lower down." These terms, and a few others, really need to be consigned to history.

You're still you, no better or worse, higher or lower, than the people around you.

5. Not realizing that you have to start learning and keep learning.

Don't believe anyone who tells you that managing is instinctive – you're born to it or you're not. I have heard this comment too often in my career and it usually comes from managers who are known to be stifling the talent around them out of insecurity. This sort of comment is also used to justify a few prejudices about who looks like a manager and who doesn't.

Management is not instinctive. It's a profession. It can be learned and anyone can improve. It can take years to become confident, and those who are genuinely good at it never pretend that it's easy. Like all professionals, managers need to understand that their learning will be ongoing. A doctor continues to keep abreast of developments, pilots go back into simulators, teachers go away for training days and sports professionals continue to work with their coaches constantly.

When people are promoted they are never told, "Obviously you know everything and there is no room for improvement." However, it's surprising how often new managers come to the conclusion that this is exactly what the promotion means. Becoming a supervisor or a leader is like joining a new school – but this one never ends. Even if you came out of Harvard Business School when you started as a manager, it won't be enough.

6. Failing to see that you have joined a profession.

Management is a profession. If you are called a "charge hand" or "foreman" or "team leader", you have still joined management and therefore you've joined a profession.

Professionalism is an attitude. It attaches itself to a person and not a title. You will encounter people who belong to what we think of as professions who do not behave professionally. It's entirely possible to find professional cleaners and unprofessional lawyers.

Professionalism in management means that there are things you can no longer do, in terms of your behavior. If you choose to do them anyway, you will certainly not be considered a professional, and the end consequences could be a lot more serious than just that.

Identify and be honest about any prejudices and negative feelings you might have about particular groups, and then do all that you can to bury those feelings while you're at work. You cannot say (or email or joke) about anything racist, sexist or ageist, or behave in a way that a reasonable person would recognize as offensive. Treat everyone with courtesy and respect, and you may find that their courteous and obliging response to you will challenge your original prejudices.

You now have to behave with decorum. There are plenty of people who lean on their corporate cultures as an excuse but, as one example, it's not acceptable for you to get blind drunk whenever the company has an occasion where alcohol is served.

And watch the whining. You can no longer complain about the company or the management in front of employees – you *are* the management. You cannot moan about people who work for you to others in the team. You cannot complain about other managers in the company to the people who report to you. This doesn't mean that you're unable to criticize anything, but your comments need to be constructive, thoughtful, and made to the appropriate people. When you need to have a good vent, call a friend. I have friends who

I can email or text various expletives about my day and it's surprisingly cathartic.

You cannot break the basic rules, or turn a blind eye to others who do. Your actions and standards will be seen as acceptable and therefore people will feel free to copy you. It is worth repeating: You are now a role model. You need to live with that.

7. *Trying to demand that people respect you.*

Not possible. Respect is earned.

8. *Trying to be everyone's best friend or mate.*

Wanting to be liked and loved is a basic human desire but it can get in the way of being a good boss. I've seen people struggle to manage because they really wanted to be one of the boys or girls.

Steven was a very capable specialist I saw being promoted to manager. Not long after the promotion he started to play up constantly and was trying to be everyone's mate. It was a noticeable change, and his new cynicism and anti-management comments were irritating the guy who had promoted him. Steven knew he wasn't coping. "I know why I keep joking around," he said. "It's because bosses were the people we always made fun of in my family. The management was the enemy and in my entire family no one ever believed they would be on that side." He hadn't told anyone in his family about his promotion. He said he could predict the reaction: "So you think you're better than us now, do you?" Steven was on the road to sabotaging the opportunity instead.

The biggest issue with trying to be mates is the inability (or great reluctance) to make difficult decisions about people. Managers have to make cutbacks and tough decisions, and they need to be able to do it in a timely fashion with fairness and objectivity. Even if you're not cutting back or dealing with serious problems you still have to say NO quite often.

It is impossible to deal with a problem employee effectively if you don't want to upset that person and their co-workers. I would like a dollar for every time I've heard a manager say "I don't want to be the bad guy." This usually follows the same manager telling me that an employee has been a problem for years.

It's not about being the bad guy.

Putting the desire to be loved and liked above effective decision-making doesn't work. "Friendly – but not friends" is a useful motto. You are no longer one of the boys or girls. You may not get invited along to everything. Sometimes the job is a bit lonely.

9. Not giving people the trust and freedom to get on with their work.

Bill is one of the best managers I have known. He is the perfect role model of professionalism, a superb team builder, and the sort of person who attracts people to his projects. He listens first and speaks later, usually to ask intelligent questions. I am not aware of him ever raising his voice. He speaks to everyone as an equal. In my view, this makes for strength in management. My own time on one of his projects was one of the best work experiences I've ever had.

He once told me that an employee approached him in his first months as a manager, and calmly and quietly said,

"Please, please stop. This really can't go on." As a result of Bill's inability to trust people to get on with their work, he was irritating the hell out of everyone.

> "I was so poor at delegating that I'd been asking people to do things and then chasing them down at ridiculously short intervals wondering why the tasks weren't done. I was hovering and looking agitated, rather than letting people get on with things. It was the first time I'd had to stand back from the technical output, and I felt pretty helpless. And as I thought I could obviously do some of these things faster, I started to panic, wondering why they hadn't finished in the time I could have taken. To make matters worse, in my state of panic, I would set someone else the same task, not having remembered that it was already delegated, or not having the confidence to chivvy the original assignee one more time. Thankfully, someone stepped forward."

This was a high-risk strategy for the employee but luckily he was talking to Bill, a guy who knows that feedback is usually intended to help, that we are never above a bit of criticism and that we learn from our mistakes.

"To add to the humiliation, this man was a design engineer and so quiet that he rarely spoke up about anything. He wore headphones at work so as not to be disturbed. Even with the sound blocked out, he'd observed the mess I was making and still had the courage to beg me to stop."

10. Not realizing that you can change.

> Any man is liable to err. Only a fool persists in error.
>
> Cicero

Bill would not be the superb manager he is today if he hadn't appreciated that gift of honest feedback and then done something about it. You only become effective by learning from your mistakes. No one is promoted to manager on the assumption that they're perfect in every way and unlikely to ever make a mistake.

His advice today is, "an early apology is not that hard to give and is a fantastic means of defusing some very heated situations. Resentment seems to fade away before your eyes when you apologize."

If you have behaved badly then you need to act. You need to do something to regain trust. You are free to apologize, make a change, ask for some support and start over. None of these things require filling out a form or getting committee approval.

Whatever you do – whether it's early days or after thirty years of managing – you can still say sorry, admit that you need some help and start over.

Thank goodness.

CHAPTER TWO

UNDERSTANDING HUMAN BEINGS

SETTING REALISTIC EXPECTATIONS ABOUT OTHER HUMAN BEINGS
WHAT DO YOU REALLY KNOW ABOUT PEOPLE?
HOW CAN YOU GET PEOPLE TO DO THE THNGS YOU NEED THEM TO DO?
THE BIG MISTAKES TO AVOID WHEN INFLUENCING OTHERS

*

SETTING REALISTIC EXPECTATIONS ABOUT OTHER HUMAN BEINGS

How can you get work done through others yet still behave like a decent human being? How do you get independent, capable people to work together and understand what's required of them, with reasonable speed, cooperation and minimal aggravation.

To begin this challenge with some chance of success, it's important to appreciate some very basic truths about human beings.

1. You cannot make people do things.

You can probably already see a conflict between having a role that asks you to get things done through others and then hearing the news that you can't force people do things.

The truth is that human beings are free to choose their own actions. This is bad news for those who want to wave a big stick and bark at people. The modern world has become a bit squeamish about bullying, aggression, slaps, threats, whips and cattle prods. We don't generally employ chain gangs or slaves anymore – and if you do, I doubt you'd be reading a book like this. The workplaces where you can get away with being an aggressive tyrant are slowly disappearing.

This is because those pesky employees are getting very good at resigning from jobs, downshifting, moving about, litigating, and altogether they're just not terribly inclined to put up with bad behavior from their bosses anymore. Actually, they were never very keen on it but these days they're more likely to vote with their feet or call in some support.

A good manager was never one who shouted and screamed all day. That was never managing in the true sense of the word. Threats and abuse were never intelligent management techniques.

Luckily most people tend to be quite cooperative in the workplace. They are smart enough to know that they're paid to produce work and the vast majority of employees take pride in doing something well. And again, luckily, the majority of employees rarely refuse to do the job they're paid to do or go out of their way to cause problems without a good reason.

2. You don't really know people.

A manager once boasted to me that "over the years I've learned to read people very quickly and I know exactly which way they're going to jump." I'm sure he's not alone in thinking that this is a sign of tremendous management competence, but it's not. It is folly and arrogance.

You can work with someone for twenty years and still not know them. You might think you do, but you're kidding yourself. All you really know is how they've behaved in front of you. Your perception of that behavior is unique. That is not the same thing as knowing how to read someone and being able to predict their behavior.

3. You do not own the people who report to you.

Another manager bragged, "I've got my team exactly where I want them. I own them. They would run through fire for me." Again – such foolish arrogance. How bizarre to imagine that this is some sign of good management. In fact, it wasn't true. His employees might well have started a fire near him, but it wouldn't have been because *they* wanted to run through it.

There's another problem with this kind of belief. Look carefully at those words: "They are where I want them." There is an underlying tone that suggests he is above those who work in his team. A good manager knows they don't own someone because of a reporting line on a chart.

If you try to manage people in a heavy-handed way, they will resist you.

Animals behave at their worst when they're cornered or threatened. So do human beings, although they may not resist you in an obvious way. They might not show their fangs and hiss at you but the desire to do it is there.

And still, you must get things done through other people.

Is it a hopeless situation? Of course not! It's ideal. You have human beings around you who can think and make choices. It's liberating and much less stressful to let go of the myth that we can predict and control people. If you stop trying to achieve the impossible it frees you to focus on the manageable world instead.

Accept the imperfect and unpredictable workplace as normal but realize that you need to be clear, organized and professional when you're dealing with people. Separate what you can influence from the things you will never control. Notice the savings you make on painkillers.

4. You can't make people like each other.

It's a bonus if employees get along but it's not critical. They have to be, at a minimum, civil, respectful and helpful. That might sound a bit cold but it's worth emphasizing this point because some managers try too hard to create family-type bonding among employees or they worry if people dislike each other.

Forcing a team atmosphere can backfire, distract you from the real business and intrude on the privacy of those people who like to keep to themselves when they're at work. Wanting compliance and constant agreement all the time is not realistic. A sea of smiley faces is also not realistic. In fact, it might be a sign of something quite disturbing.

5. There are no perfect days. Be content with "good enough".

If you stop expecting perfect days, the role becomes less stressful and more interesting. It's tempting to believe that we would have good days if only people did as they were told, if only customers stopped being difficult or if only all employees were star performers. It's not going to happen.

In *The Paradox of Choice*, author Barry Schwartz puts it differently:

"I make a distinction between people we call maximizers, people who always need to get the best, and satisfiers, those who are satisfied with good enough. We find consistently that maximizers are miserable."

Management is an art, not an exact science. We can't apply a theory or model to employees and expect to get a consistent, predictable response. Give up on any notion that there is a simple answer out there that will take all the people problems away. There isn't. People are not able to be programmed, no matter how many times you watch *The Manchurian Candidate* to pick up tips. Behavior breeds behavior. That's about the most we can be sure of.

So what can you do?

You can do a great deal. First of all, you can:

- understand some basics about influencing people.
- understand that your own behavior is a powerful role model and that the things you pay attention to (or ignore) are important.
- learn to delegate real work as part of an ongoing plan.

- listen so that people will let you know what's going on and be easy approaching you.
- talk to people as equals and make things as clear as you possibly can.
- understand the importance of your words, actions and attention in getting people's enthusiasm and commitment.
- do everything within your power to stay calm.
- find people who are likely to be a good match for the tasks you need doing.
- create a work atmosphere that helps you keep good employees interested.
- learn to let people go, especially those who are really hindering the results.
- gain some confidence in dealing with the issues of conflict and change that will inevitably arise.

This list helps to form the structure and content of the rest of this book so let's start at the very top.

WHAT DO YOU REALLY KNOW ABOUT PEOPLE?

I know that there are plenty of decent managers in the world who understand the basics about dealing with human beings. I am also too familiar with managers who speak of their employees as something less than human, who completely fail to see or credit basic needs and feelings in their staff and then search for some miracle to fix their people problems.

Managers are people who need people. You will succeed as a manager if people choose to help you rather than hinder you. The root causes of failure and success in business are all to do with human behavior. Everything else is a symptom.

Although people are different and changeable, certain things remain fairly constant. Consider your own feelings and how you liked to be managed and see if this list makes sense to you.

1. *We like recognition and attention.*

We like respect. We like someone to look at us when they're talking to us. Please and thank you are valued words and we notice their absence keenly. The cheapest and easiest fix for poor managers and destructive teams is to start using good manners as a habit.

2. *We do not like ridicule and embarrassment.*

When criticism is necessary, we appreciate a boss who can give the message constructively, sticking to the relevant point and not making the mistake of attacking us as people. We would prefer this to be done quietly, in private if possible, with a boss who can stay calm. We may react very badly when criticized in front of other employees or customers.

> *The important things in life are love, sex,*
> *death and the avoidance of humiliation.*
> Sue Townsend, author.

3. *We dislike rejection.*

We don't like being excluded, ignored, or treated like a fool. We love being asked for our opinion. We can be incredibly helpful, cooperative and capable if our boss makes it a habit to ask our opinion and acknowledge our contributions.

4. We like to have some control over our lives.

Some of us like a lot of control and some want a little. It's true that some employees may say they just want to be told what to do, but don't be fooled by that. What you may be hearing is actually the result of a lifelong exclusion from having any say in the workplace, or a mildly distressed employee who is suddenly being asked for an opinion, for a change. Or it may be someone who has no faith whatsoever that what they say will be heard, let alone acted upon. They are tired. They have given up.

So make sure you ask people for their thoughts on work matters, especially about those aspects of work that affect them directly. You might not get a response every time, you might want to give people time to think and come back to you, but invariably people like to be asked. In any case, you're likely to make better decisions if you have all the facts before you.

You will encounter cynicism and irritation if people decide this consultation is phony and that you've already made the decision.

5. What motivates and satisfies one person may not float the boat of another.

Human beings are usually wondering "What's in it for *me?*" The answer varies widely. We move in the direction that satisfies our own unique set of needs. Our needs can change too.

For example, most people need attention and feedback and the amount that is deemed enough can vary. Ask a group of people "How much money is enough?" and you'll see what

I mean. Or watch a buffet table in an All You Can Eat place and ponder how much food is enough for some.

Good managers try to marry up tasks and business goals with what an employee might want from the situation. This is not a simple thing to do. There's an entire chapter on this coming up called "Keeping People."

6. We share some common emotions.

We all feel anger, sadness, fear and joy, but we have very different ways of showing those feelings. We need to have these basic emotions in order to be healthy human beings. We don't check these emotions into a locker as we arrive at work. Most of us are conditioned to behave in a fairly neutral way while we're at work, but never assume that emotions are far from the surface of anyone you are dealing with. They bubble away, disrupting our thoughts and affecting our decisions constantly.

7. People are quite fond of habit and consistency.

Human beings are not generally fond of changing the status quo. They need a good reason to do that. Some people can resist change, even if it's of great benefit to them. The known world can get very comfortable. Even a bad habit may be clung to. Introducing change is likely to elicit a push back because "the way things are" is being challenged.

Having said that, we are remarkably resilient too, and while we can react negatively to change, over time, we endure a great deal of it. (And Managing Change takes up a section later in this book.)

8. People see things very differently and come to different conclusions and decisions as a consequence.

Our perspective is unique. So is our sense of proportion. For example, consider this nightmare experienced by Andrew Cavendish, 11th Duke of Devonshire: "I had a terrible day two years ago when the Duke of Marlborough's grapes beat mine at the fruit show, and I got back to my club to read in the *Evening Standard* that the Duke of Beaufort was now the best dressed duke."

I do hope he was joking. If you've ever seen the house Andrew Cavendish inherited at Chatsworth in the UK, you would have some difficulty feeling sorry for him and his runner-up grapes.

There's a large filing cabinet in the human mind labeled: This is how the world is. It has a very different set of contents for every human being.

Everyone has a self-image or an inner voice that says "This is who I am." This self-image is a very powerful influence on behavior. A person may have an image of themselves that is inconsistent with reality. The self-image can be a stronger and more determined noise than anything you as a manager might have to say. You may perceive an employee to have tremendous ability, and they may try to talk you out of that opinion. The reverse can also happen.

Reality and truth are subjects that would take up a vast amount of time in a philosophy course, but for this chapter, just let me say that you will never have a group of people who view a situation the same way. Send an email to twenty people and there will be at least twenty interpretations of it.

9. *You can observe a person's behavior. You do not know their personality.*

It has been said that we know more about outer space than we do about the functioning of the human brain. We do not know, for certain, whether people are completely free to make decisions. Psychologists and scientists have long argued over whether we are born to behave in certain ways or if we are shaped by our upbringing.

But a good boss doesn't need to know the personalities of those who work with them. This is handy since we can't really know personalities anyway and psychologists can't seem to agree on a definition either.

What you can freely discuss is behavior – the things a person says and does. Confine yourself to discussions about the things that employees say and do, or the results they produce or fail to produce. Behavior is observable and often quantifiable. If I am set a task to fetch ten boxes, you'd know if I did or did not do it.

I could write a great deal more about people and their behavior and every sentence could be debated. Understanding people is an ongoing challenge for all managers. It's not important that you have a degree in psychology before you manage a team but it is important that you appreciate the need to have insight into your own behavior and interpersonal skills.

It's also worth repeating that you'll never be an expert and there will always be surprises. Good managers who have been around for a while are more likely to say "The more I learn, the more I realize the less I know."

HOW CAN YOU GET PEOPLE TO DO THE THINGS YOU NEED THEM TO DO?

You don't control people, but as a manager, you do have a very strong influence on their behavior. People decide their reactions and they can choose to follow a leader.

So how do you get them to make this choice in favor of your needs?

Shaping and influencing behavior means getting familiar with the principles of modeling and reinforcement. Modeling and reinforcement is how most of us learn skills and habits. It is how toddlers learn to use a knife and fork and teenagers learn to drive. It's also the most effective way of getting things done through the efforts of others.

Modeling

We have a habit of copying. We tend to set our own behavior to the standard around us, and so your behavior as a boss is very potent. It can help to influence a good working environment. It can also be incredibly destructive and the major contributor to low morale. Both are possible.

You are a role model and the way you behave matters a great deal. The things you pay attention to will tend to be repeated. There is a double-edged effect in this and I will explain it further on in this chapter.

Parents who observe their children are not surprised by the concept of modeling, or the power of it. Most parents have cringed at some time to hear their children repeat something inappropriate, knowing exactly where they picked it up from. It's not hard to see how quickly children copy someone they admire or the behavior of friends and siblings.

Adults remain adept copiers of behavior. Think about the way we can fall into line with the walking step of the person we're with, or just mirror their body language whether it's relaxed or more formal. Think about how we can copy the speech patterns of people in our conversations. If the person we're talking to is relaxed or loud or swearing, it can give us license to copy them. The reverse can also occur. If someone is well spoken, we tend to lift our game.

It hits some bosses like a bolt of lightning that the reason they keep seeing problems or habits from their staff is because their staff are simply mirroring or copying them. Behavior breeds behavior.

When you think about it, it's quite rational to copy the boss's behavior because

- it's likely to get positive attention from the boss, and we like that.
- it gets positive attention from others if our behavior fits in.
- we might want to become like the boss to have what the boss has.
- we see fitting in as a key to survival.

We copy the boss because it answers the basic question, "What am I supposed to do?" and surely the boss must know.

We copy good and bad examples of behavior.

We can also adjust our behavior to what everyone else is doing, even though it doesn't make us particularly happy. Human beings like to conform and connect. That's why some destructive, thoughtless or dangerous habits can spread. If the workplace is miserable, people can copy miserable behaviors and adapt to that environment because it's the model that is all around them, and being different might become tiring. Think about how hard it is to remain cheerful or positive if you're constantly spending time with grim people.

Why do employees tend to copy the boss and not the person who delivers the spare parts? The answer is not just because the boss is there more often, it's because they are an authority figure. Like it or not, people are looking at you as the standard setter, the key person whose actions spell out "this is the way it is, this is what's acceptable."

We may search for special motivational tricks when in fact, one of the best ways to influence the behavior of others is simply to take a long, hard look in the mirror and then change our own behavior.

To get the modeling part right you need to start by asking yourself:

- What do I want to see this person (or this team) doing?
- Am I upholding that standard of behavior myself?
- Have I explained very clearly what is needed and why?
- Have I shown an example of what the end result should be?

And then you need to be the model of the behavior you want to see.

- If you want people to stay calm under pressure, then you have to stay calm.
- If you want people to work safely and stop what they're doing if there is a safety risk, then you have to work safely and respect a halt for safety.

- If you want people to resolve a conflict in an adult manner, then you have to be someone who behaves in a calm and constructive manner during a conflict.
- If you want to see a bit of enthusiasm ... well you know how it goes.

Actions have always spoken louder than words. It's absolutely pointless to demand and expect of others what you're not doing yourself.

Some examples of mixed messages:

- Demanding attention to detail but working in a slapdash manner yourself.
- Asking to see interest and energy but acting like a cynical sloth.
- Expecting people to work as a team but being known as someone who only takes care of themselves.

It's never worked well, on four year olds or forty-four year olds, to be told "Don't worry about what I do. You just do as I say."

Modeling is also, very importantly, about telling and showing people what to do.

I've heard managers complain that an employee will not do something that is expected of them or will not behave in a certain way. And yet the important conversation, the very clear conversation about exactly what is expected, has never taken place. So the employee has never really seen or understood what the boss is talking about.

Why has this talk been avoided? The answer is often somewhere between "Well, they ought to know" and "No one ever told me" and "They're grown-ups, aren't they?"

I guess we ought to know a lot of things, but we don't. We need to learn. We need some help. Left to our own devices we may have to guess what is wanted or else copy from someone else who works near us.

Don't leave people to guess what they're supposed to do and the standard of quality required. Tell people what you're looking for. Make sure they're shown how to do the task. The time you take to clearly explain work and help people to get it right will be time well spent, and the investment will pay off many times over. A good boss is constantly aiming to develop independent, capable people who can get on with their work.

Reinforcement

A builder uses the term reinforcement to mean strengthen. In management terms, reinforcement is also about strengthening. You are trying to strengthen a behavior until it becomes a habit, and just like modeling, this process is occurring anyway whether you like it or not.

If modeling is largely about leading by example, then reinforcement is mostly about how you react to people's behavior. It's about what happens next. Your attention can reinforce good behavior or help it to go away. Whether behavior goes away may be a good or a bad thing.

Think about what happens in your work team when someone does something right. Do you pay attention in a positive way, a negative manner, or ignore what has just happened?

Of course, you're not always watching, and you can't spend your day reacting to everyone, but reinforcement requires some level of reaction. What small acts or changes do you often see that are moving in the right direction?

Good bosses learn to catch people doing right. This means that you need to observe performance, but you should be doing that in a general sense anyway as part of everyday leading and controlling. Behavior that gets rewarded with attention is likely to be repeated.

When someone produces the result you wanted, the smart thing to do is to react fairly quickly with positive reinforcement. That could mean a "thank you", "great" or a "cheers" or some quick sign that clearly shows the person that they did the right thing. A smile, head nod or a thumbs-up gesture can be read as positive reinforcement. Giving someone your time and attention, taking an interest, helping a person to acquire a useful skill, or simply explaining how their work fits into the bigger picture, are also very simple ways that a boss can positively reinforce good work.

Employees who look slightly stunned when hearing positive reinforcement or feel inclined to make suspicious remarks are not telling you they dislike the praise. They're telling you that it's been a long time since they heard any and they're not sure if it's a wind-up. If they fall down and need to be revived, then they're really saying that you've been unusually stingy with positive reinforcement.

Obviously good behavior can be positively reinforced with tangible rewards such as money, promotions, prizes, trips, perks and benefits. People can certainly become cheesed off if there is an imbalance, shortage or lack of fairness in the way these tangible rewards are given out. Tangible rewards do matter, but they only represent part of the story.

While a simple "thank you", "great job" or "good one" cannot be cashed in at the bank, this kind of quick and positive response is extremely powerful. You need to use whatever simple terms of appreciation are expressed comfortably in your culture.

Understanding just how valued these simple gestures of appreciation are to the receiver helps us understand why some folk leave high-paying jobs, switch between high-paying companies, flock to the voluntary sector, or just feel miserable in jobs and work places that we might think look pretty cushy.

To say it again – we really like recognition. We like genuine, sincere, relevant praise for doing something right, regardless of our age, IQ or profession. If you don't believe me, listen in on a group of disgruntled workers. The top gripe will often be that "no one ever tells you that you've done a good job." We notice reinforcement when it's missing. Unhappy workplaces are often devoid of encouragement or basic manners.

But no one likes positive reinforcement if it comes across as smarmy, insincere, over the top, irrelevant, or applied to absolutely everyone. Free-floating praise causes worried looks. A loudly broadcasted and shallow "Heya guys, you're doin' a great job there!" will not go down well in most workplaces. (Well, none that I've ever worked in.)

The excessive or inappropriate use of praise can also backfire. I once heard a supervisor racing around a hotel lobby telling every employee he encountered they were awesome. The Grand Canyon is awesome. An employee is rarely awesome, and would be unlikely to feel awesome if they heard all their colleagues being described with the same word within the same hour.

You must also be aware of timing. Don't tell someone a year after a great effort that they did well. It really is too late, and reinforcement that arrives late can feel pointless and annoying.

It's always better to tell your employees that they're valued before someone else does. When they've handed in their notice, you're too late.

People move in the direction of positive attention. We seek praise and encouragement. We like to believe that what we've done has made a difference.

We do not need positive reinforcement all day long for every single thing we do, but from time to time it is basic nourishment. It's also basic guidance, and ultimately, it makes the job of managing so much easier.

What about the behavior or results you don't want to see?

Negative reinforcement is any feedback or response which is likely to hurt, and I don't mean that it needs to hurt greatly or physically. The slightest emotional "ouch" is enough. Even constructive negative feedback given expertly still hurts a bit unless the receiver is unusually insensitive. No one loves hearing that they made a mistake or that they're on the wrong track but rational people can handle being corrected if it's done by a boss who is calm, clear, and able to explain what should be done instead.

To get negative reinforcement right:

- be very specific and stick to observable things.
- address the current issue, and say why it was a problem.
- never label the person. For example, it's not so bad to say "that wasn't a smart thing to do" but you should never say "you're stupid." The first statement attacks the behavior, the second attacks the person. There's a world of difference. Ideally, you wouldn't be using that first statement very often either.

Feedback that is negative but given constructively and clearly, and designed to help will be accepted. Constructive criticism is about guiding people and building on effort. Did they do anything right? If they did some good things, tell them very clearly about the good stuff because you don't want them to stop doing right.

A good boss generally tries to give credit to the person who has made a mistake because most screw-ups are not deliberate. Generally speaking, most people try to do things right and want to do well. Sometimes they're trying too hard. Ask yourself, was it a willful mistake? Was it a malicious thing? The answer most of the time is no.

You may have to spell out a consequence if the behavior is repetitive, and you'll have to mean it. If you promise to do something next time you'd better follow through, or else people will learn very quickly that your warnings and promises are meaningless.

And just like positive reinforcement, we spoil negative reinforcement if it's insincere and not related to anything specific. The timing matters just as much, so it's unwise to tell someone six months later that they've done badly. And please, never *ever* give negative feedback in front of other people. That is a standard that every manager must abide by.

The more people are used to your good opinion, trust, and encouragement, the less you have to do and say to make the point that something is wrong. A raised eyebrow may be enough, especially if you're a calm, steady kind of boss who runs a dignified workplace.

Turning a blind eye

There are three kinds of reinforcement or attention: positive, negative, and doing nothing.

Ignoring behavior, or turning a blind eye, can be a useful strategy and, as odd as it sounds, it's still a reaction you might choose to employ. This is where psychology and wise grandparents join forces.

We know that behavior that receives attention is likely to be repeated. The principle at work of ignoring behavior is that behavior that receives no pay-off or attention at all is likely to go away. The behavior is likely to atrophy for want of attention.

Since human beings seek attention as a reward, giving negative attention can also be seen as a pay-off or reward. Therefore, doing *nothing* might make the behavior disappear since no reward was given and there is no incentive to continue the behavior.

Older and sometimes wiser folk have often learned that naughty behavior from children is largely to do with seeking attention. They know that rewarding bad behavior with attention just perpetuates the problem. Look at how often an older person or grandparent will say under their breath, when confronted by naughty behavior, "Just ignore it. Don't make a fuss." Observe how often that strategy works.

Using this tactic of ignoring can make behavior go away, but be very careful. Because good behavior that gets no attention is also likely to go away as well.

People dislike negative reinforcement, but the thing human beings really cannot cope with is being ignored. Think about it. The most soul destroying of human situations is isolation, not even being seen or acknowledged. The opposite of love is indifference, rather than hatred. The opposite of feedback and attention is silence.

When the circumstance warrants a negative reaction, a manager has to decide and think clearly. Is this a good employee who has made a mistake and obviously will not do this as a habit? Is this a big deal? Is this a safety issue? Is this something others might copy? As a manager you are constantly juggling those kinds of decisions – what deserves praise, what deserves constructive criticism, and what can safely be ignored.

People make mistakes. If you jump at everything you will be in danger of nitpicking, and that is demoralizing.

For example, an employee is always on time but one morning their bus breaks down and they're late. You call them aside to have strong words about timekeeping.

How do you think they feel? Where is their motivation right now? (Where would yours be?)

If a problem persists or escalates and you've tried ignoring it, then you may have to give some constructive feedback. Always stop and consider the situation with a cool head and try to avoid reacting in the heat of the moment. Thoughtful managers make decisions about reactions and pay-offs all the time.

THE BIG MISTAKES TO AVOID WHEN INFLUENCING OTHERS

1. We don't give positive feedback because we think we might sound weird.

I've heard managers dismiss the whole concept of positive reinforcement by ridiculing it as "that fluffy stuff." The same managers will often complain that morale is low in their team or that they can't find good people. They wonder why employees have no loyalty these days.

Some bosses bristle at the idea of giving someone a positive word at all. We can make excuses such as "they'd think that was weird" or "that's just not part of the culture."

Employees don't expect weekly bunches of flowers and ritual group hugs. Consider the realistic needs of the people around you.

2. We think we're too busy.

I was once told by a manager on a training program that "saying thank you isn't possible. I'm too busy."

One of his colleagues became angry and said, "That's pathetic. If someone does a good job, you just tell them 'Thanks mate, I appreciate it.' It takes a second."

The group was of a scientific disposition and happy to time the difference with a second hand on a watch. Of course, there is no time in it at all.

You're not being asked to write a speech or design an appreciation award. "I'm too busy" or "There's no time" really is a pathetic excuse.

3. We worry that in giving someone positive feedback they might manipulate us or immediately ask for a pay rise.

Another excuse for withholding praise is this: "What if they come back with a demand for more money?"

Think about it. Is that realistic? Have you ever behaved this way in response to some positive feedback? Have you seen others do this? Are we really working in places where people instantly seize upon a "thank you" or a "well done" as an excuse to ask for money on the spot?

4. *We nitpick and only look for the problems.*

Imagine cooking someone a five-course meal and preparing a table with candles, wine and flowers. At the end of this meal, having made no comment or gesture of appreciation, your guest mumbles, "The peas were a bit cold."

How much would you feel like inviting them back and putting in that effort again?

Consider the demoralizing effect of the nitpicker boss who ignores all the good things you do but finds fault in some tiny aspect of the work. Nitpickers create flat, uninspiring work environments.

5. *We devalue the positive remarks by overdoing them, applying them to everyone or making it all too weak.*

Overdoing praise by providing someone with positive feedback all the time and for the simplest things will either breed cynicism or produce very confused employees.

Congratulating everyone in the team for a great effort is fine, but have you just praised the guy who's been loafing? How will that feel for the people who did the good work?

Vague cheery comments to a large group can be a bit lame. It doesn't tell people exactly what they did well and it might sound as if you don't really know.

Praising teams is OK, but people are individuals and a bit egocentric. There's nothing quite as powerful as feedback that is given directly.

On the subject of weak reinforcement, I've known of managers who tried to build positive feedback into their working week by scheduling a time in their diary to walk about and praise everyone. Staff quickly cottoned on to what was happening and the managers, who had good intentions, became a laughing stock. You need to make it real and spontaneous.

6. We devalue the negative remarks by shouting and yelling all the time.

Most people can handle constructive feedback, and even the negatives, if they are delivered in the right way, but no one's going to take you seriously if you're known for yelling and making demeaning comments.

Over time, the people you need to listen to you will develop a thick skin. The danger is that their skin becomes so thick, they tune you out permanently. How handy will that be when you need to get something really important across?

If you fly off the handle as a habit, how will you make the point when you are genuinely concerned and something is seriously wrong? Everyone will start to take your hysterics with a pinch of salt. People become immune to the volume and the gestures. You'll have to become louder and more hysterical to make your point. Consider what that will do to your own health. We all know what it does to morale.

You're also tempting revenge. People do not like to be humiliated or put down, especially in front of others. They will get their own back. Naive bosses think sabotage is only about damaged equipment or vandalism, but sabotage can be inflicted in a thousand ways and in forms that you might not be able to see or understand. Simply withholding our best effort, keeping solutions and ideas to ourselves and failing to be helpful are some common forms of sabotage. Ask angry employees to tell you how they have wrought revenge on a boss they loathed, and you will learn just how creative people can be in the art of sabotage.

If something has gone wrong then focus on the problem. Put your energy into finding a solution. The more people are used to your professional behavior and steady demeanor, the less you need to do to impart criticism and correct performance. If you show your frustration for good reason, on rare occasions and without being personally abusive, then people are far more likely to sit up and take note.

7. We don't realize that all behavior which gets rewarded with attention is likely to be repeated, even the bad behavior.

Following on from the previous point, overdoing the shouting at people has consequences that some employees will enjoy. The naive boss asks "Are you suggesting they're winding me up deliberately?" You get what you pay attention to. We are all attention-seeking creatures. Even the best bosses must face the prospect that certain individuals actively look for negative reinforcement as a way of getting attention.

8. We think – why should I?

The "Why should I thank someone for doing something they're paid to do?" comment often pops up as a reason to avoid praising anyone. And I have frequently heard this kind of boss also complaining, "Well, no one ever thanks me." So this manager notices the absence of positive feedback himself – and clearly doesn't feel great about it.

Behavior breeds behavior.

There are some bosses who believe that giving praise or credit where it's due incurs a painful cost to them. The objection is "Why should I?" They've never seen a compliment as an investment or just an easy, humane thing to do. I often feel a bit sad hearing this response. I'm sure their attitude is affecting other relationships. What goes around comes around, and then they wonder why no one praises or encourages them.

Why should you give praise and credit? It will save you time and effort in the long run. The effect of higher morale impacts on your bottom line in productivity and safety, but a kinder, more thoughtful workplace is a good enough reason.

No one ever hands you any positive feedback? That's a shame, but why not break the cycle of meanness and become a better boss than the one you're reporting to?

9. We hope the problem will go away.

A good boss will not ignore something that impacts on security, the law, health and safety, or any behavior that is deemed to be "gross misconduct".

In health and safety you need to set very clear rules and follow through on discipline. You can't ignore financial abuses, theft, assault, drug and alcohol breaches, and anything that you would consider to be gross misconduct. Ignore these breaches of standards at your peril.

You may occasionally find yourself in a situation where the small problem you turned a blind eye to has now become worse. Perhaps other employees have joined in through imitation. It's time to act.

Sometimes managers hope the problem will go away because they don't wish to confront someone they like, or because they're afraid of them or their connections. That's not sustainable for any business.

It's not unusual to find managers putting off necessary negative feedback because the situation is painful or embarrassing. There are conversations most of us would rather avoid, but there is more help with having these talks in the next chapter.

10. *We ignore good behavior and it goes away.*

One of the biggest mistakes managers make is that they do nothing when people do good work. They unknowingly punish people with silence and to a human being, this is worse than criticism. At least criticism can be counted as attention.

In trying to create a positive work climate you might think that leaving a good employee alone is a healthy, motivating thing to do and indicates that you trust them.

There are certainly people who are more self-motivated and independent than others and whose needs are small in terms of attention. But no one likes to work for a long time without any positive comment or recognition for good effort.

Talk to an independent good performer who is being ignored and I will guarantee that the lack of reinforcement is chipping away at their motivation. Often this person will say "You never hear a word when you're doing the right thing, but you make a mistake and boy, do you hear about it."

If we ignore people who come up with good ideas, then it won't take long for that person and everyone else to learn "Don't bother."

When employees say they like to be given freedom, it usually means that they like to make decisions and get on without unnecessary interference. It doesn't mean that they like their achievements and contributions to be taken for granted.

11. We worry they will become too confident.

This reaction is typified by the question: "But won't they get a big head if I praise them?" Why worry so much about building confidence? Isn't that what a good manager ought to do?

I heard this kind of objection from a manager who said that she was in an employee's market and therefore positive reinforcement wasn't possible. "I don't want to let them know they're doing well or they might think they've got a good chance of getting a job somewhere else," she said. She preferred to let her staff carry on believing they were incompetent and there was no market for their skills.

Employees are free to leave you at any time but if you are the encouraging type, they might conclude that they have found a place to succeed in, and stay with you.

So what is the best chance of getting someone to behave the way you want them to?

- Decide what kind of behavior you want to see from people.
- Demonstrate that behavior consistently yourself.
- Tell people what you want, and why it matters.
- Teach them if necessary. Train, coach, explain and show.
- When you observe the right thing, reward it. That doesn't necessarily mean money. Acknowledgement and praise are highly valued.

- When you see behavior you don't want, ignore it if you can. It might be a one-off.
- If you can't ignore it, decide why it matters. Talk to the person about it. Stay calm. Don't insult people or make a huge fuss. If it's very serious or more than a one-off, then look at the chapter coming up called "Letting People Go."
- Repeat this process constantly.

The goal is to establish a habit. After a short while we do not need constant reinforcement every time we do a task right because doing the job the right way has become a habit.

Be careful that you don't over-manage.

When it comes to shaping behavior a manager must stay focused on what they are paid to do. Stick to the results that you and the team are trying to achieve. Trying to shape people to be safer at work, better skilled, more effective or more accurate, are reasonable goals to aim for. But resist trying to change people's values, lifestyles or general demeanor.

You'll always have some whiners, some negative types, some who get too enthusiastic and carried away, and some people who have ideas and behaviors that you don't particularly like. Some will be ambitious, and some will not. Some will have stable home lives and some will have personal problems that will make your hair curl.

For example, a manager asked me how she could use modeling and reinforcement principles to influence an employee who was refusing to join any social functions.

"Maybe he doesn't want to join in," I suggested.

"But he just keeps to himself," she said. "We ask him out to our lunches and coffees and he always says no."

"He's allowed to do that," I said.

"But this is a teamwork issue and he's not cooperating!"

In fact, it's not a teamwork issue unless he's obstructing the work he's paid to do. Where is it written in his contract or his performance agreement that he has to participate in office social functions? A contract for employment doesn't allow us to interfere in someone's free time to this degree.

Another manager was far more pragmatic. He had employees doing the sort of work that most of us would never want. "We don't make any demands on people to talk about their lives or histories," he told me. "Many of our workers are passing through. They keep to themselves and are often in difficult personal situations. Quite a few will have a criminal record of some kind."

He encouraged employees to work as a team so as to be clear about who was doing what, and to communicate sufficiently to stay safe. If they didn't want to organize a social club, he was never going to suggest it.

This is an important point, because we must be clear about what we need to address and what we can let go. This is what all managers must decide.

The rational goal for any boss in shaping behavior is to get people do the job they're paid to do to the standard you want them to do it. If they're pleasant, happy people with enthusiasm then that's a bonus.

CHAPTER THREE

COMMUNICATING

How to talk and listen to people so that people will want to talk and listen to you

LISTENING TO PEOPLE
TALKING TO PEOPLE
FIVE THINGS EVERY MANAGER CAN DO TO IMPROVE THE WAY THEY COMMUNICATE
HANDLING UNPLEASANT CONVERSATIONS

*

LISTENING TO PEOPLE

The sad truth is that most of us don't listen all that well. We hear people, but we might not be paying close attention to what they're saying. We may not make a genuine effort to understand them.

Fran Lebowitz, columnist and social observer, wrote "The opposite of talking isn't listening. The opposite of talking is waiting." Hearing and listening are not the same things. You can hear someone without really listening to them.

When we're tired, busy, bored, or just feel we've heard the same thing a million times, it's a challenge to really listen to another person. Good listening, or "active listening" is a drain on our energy even when we're quite good at it. And yet active listening is a skill that managers must have in their toolkit in order to be effective as leaders. Money is wasted on leadership development, coaching and mentoring if the skill of listening is not addressed.

Why does active listening get so little attention? I suspect it's because it lacks the glitter of the next big theory of management. Consultants are often handed large checks for writing reports when some active listening within the business would have yielded the same information.

You have to actively listen when someone has an idea, a problem, an opinion or an answer. You also need to listen actively when a mistake has been made, something must be explained, when someone wants to talk about their work, needs technical advice, or wants to share a personal problem that may be affecting their work. If you fail to listen at these key moments, employees will quickly learn not to bother you and you may start wondering why no one ever tells you anything.

If you cannot listen, then how will people tell you what they need, what's going well, and what isn't? How will you plan if you don't listen to advice about the business, the future, and what is reasonable? How will you make decisions when you don't have all the necessary information? How will you get any instructions, let alone your overall plans across if people block you out? And they will do that if they believe you've blocked them. Put simply, **if you cannot listen, then you can't be successful in the role of boss.**

Getting it wrong

These are some of the typical signs of poor listening from managers:

- Exhaling in a bored way or doing a kind of shoulder slump when your employee tries to tell you something.
- Looking irritated, glancing at your watch or phone, or keeping busy with another task like email, when someone is trying to talk to you.
- Answering your phone as soon as it rings, without even apologizing for picking it up.
- Walking away when someone is talking to you.
- Interrupting frequently or instantly dismissing whatever they're saying.

Getting it right

Employees who speak highly of their managers commonly say that he or she "pays attention." "They listen to what you've got to say." "You feel comfortable talking to them." Charismatic leaders are often known for making you feel like you're the only person in the room.

The good news is that active listening is a skill that can be developed. The most important starting point is to hold back the inner urge to stick in your two cents' worth when someone is talking to you. That's a lot easier said than done. There's a human urge that compels many of us to compete in conversations to exercise control or win the point.

Active listening forces us to focus on the other person and strive to understand what they're saying. They must be the priority in the conversation. This is a new concept for some of us – taking a genuine interest in another person might be unfamiliar territory.

Active listening requires that you face someone and look at them. Stop what you're doing – particularly typing, texting, or walking in the opposite direction. Balance this with a respectful physical distance and make sure you're not glaring at them. Eye contact should be appropriate – neither intense nor darting all over the place. Look at the person, not at your feet and not at your screen. And then be quiet.

- Look as if you're listening. Nod every now and then.
- Really hold back your own desire to jump in and take over. Silently remind yourself to shut up.
- Briefly summarize what is being said to you. Just do this now and then and not after every sentence. It shows that you've understood, and it proves to the other person that you're listening.
- Don't be afraid to ask a question to guide the conversation, but make sure it's relevant.

Practice is going to pay off, as it does with any skill. Find someone you trust who can help you get better at actively listening. Sometimes a manager really is listening but gives the impression that they're not. Getting help with body language is crucial.

The unfortunate bosses are those who feel that listening and showing patience is a sign of weakness, and that shutting people down and dominating conversations shows everyone who's in charge. If we worry more about status and ego, then the way we speak to people will suffer, and our willingness to genuinely listen will be low or non-existent.

Some other dos and don'ts

- If someone wants to talk and it's inconvenient, say so politely and then promise to come back when you do have the time. And commit to that promise.
- Try to hold back from jumping in quickly with "Well I think" or "I find" or "You know what you should do ..."
- If you're talking on the phone you have to sound as if you're listening. Use verbal cues like "aha."
- Never answer a ringing phone or allow another person to interrupt when someone is talking to you, unless it is urgent. If you absolutely must be interrupted, then apologize for it.
- Close the conversation with a simple thank you, an acknowledgement of what's been said, a next step or a commitment of some kind. Silence, dead air and blank expressions can cause problems. This is when colleagues might walk away and shake their head, saying, "It's like talking to a brick wall." You may have listened but they don't know that.

If you listen to people, then it's far more likely that they'll listen to you. That's a critical trade-off for a boss who needs to get things done through others.

TALKING TO PEOPLE

If you want to be a good boss, you also need to think carefully about the *way* you speak to people – not just the content, but the tone and the behavior you use in your everyday conversations.

Talking down to people aggressively

The common trap that a lot of bosses can fall into is talking down to people. The worst kind of talking down is the aggressive, dominating, insulting style that is sadly still out there in the workplace. The nickname for older managers who use this style is "Dinosaur." This is not entirely accurate – barking at people may be outdated but it's not extinct yet. It's still around because younger managers taking up the role of supervisor, foreman or manager, copy the style of managers they've had, mistakenly believing that this is what managers must do in order to get things done. The fact that they're likely to be struggling with high turnover, low morale and obstinate behavior will usually be attributed to "people these days" rather than the rod they've made for their own backs.

A worst-case example of this humiliating aggression would be a man I worked near that I'll call Stan. Stan would never use names; he'd shout "Hey you" or "Oy you" to get someone's attention. He shouted even when the employee was standing in front of him. He believed that it was useful "to tear a strip off everyone now and then because it sends a message." He was right about that. It certainly sent a message – just not the kind of message he believed he was sending.

Stan believed his staff could be excluded from all the usual common courtesies because he insisted "they're just here for the money – they don't care." He'd use phrases like "the pond life" when talking about his employees, sometimes when they were close enough to hear.

Other pet phrases that could be from Stan (and the other Stans of the working world I've encountered) include:

- "What the hell do you think you're doing?"
- "Do you think you're clever?"
- "If you had a brain you'd be dangerous."
- "What are you staring at?"
- "Did I ask for your opinion?"
- "Get back to work!"
- "Who do you think you are?"
- "Don't you tell me how to run this place."
- "Don't answer me back, boy! Who do you think you're talking to?"

And then, believe it or not ...

- "What is *wrong* with people these days?"

Stan's favorite conversational gesture was pointing a finger at someone's chest while shouting. When Stan was listening to someone – and that was a rare event – his arms were folded and he wore an "Oh yeah?" kind of expression.

Animals behave at their worst when cornered and threatened. The same goes for human beings. We do not like being threatened or spoken down to. It gets our backs up. It does not win our cooperation or inspire us to give our best, unless we're in a very unhealthy place in our lives.

The price paid for talking down to people and pushing them around is invariably sabotage. Sabotage is not just about broken machinery and obvious damage. Sabotage is more commonly about ensuring that the manager does not succeed in what they're trying to do.

People hinder your objectives by working slowly, holding back ideas and solutions, willfully making the same mistake over and over, doing the absolute minimum to stay out of trouble, and generally making sure effort is withheld wherever possible. Few of us cooperate in the long run with a manager who treats us badly. We won't necessarily quit the job, in fact we may hang around for our own reasons, but we're very unlikely to give our best.

Stan had a small group of employees who were hell-bent on sticking around to see him fail and be fired. They did everything possible to create mistakes and problems that would reflect badly on Stan in order to hurry that day along. In the meantime, Stan was often at the scene of some very suspicious near misses, and no one could ever be found to blame.

Whenever I'm training and have shared the connection I've observed with Stan-like behavior and safety in the workplace, people often tell me their own stories of their "Stans" and workplace accidents, near misses, and pranks that have been entirely centered around getting revenge. They tend to do this quietly, often during a coffee break, and it becomes something of a confession.

The full picture on this would be very hard to obtain, for obvious reasons, but I have no doubt this is one of the greatest risks being run by the Dinosaur managers who continue to talk down to people and don't seem to know a better way to get things done.

Talking down in a nice way

The other danger is talking down to employees in an indulgent, sweet and overly nurturing tone, even where it is meant kindly. In other words – the road to hell is paved with good intentions.

Far from bullying, this boss often talks as if they want to take care of people. Unfortunately, if you swing too far and overdo the niceness you start patronizing people, behaving in a mother hen way, calling them "my boys" or "my girls", and generally protecting them from full responsibility and development. Even though it sounds a lot better, it's still talking *down*. It still gets people's backs up, and they still react badly, although they may not bristle with anger and indignation.

I have in mind a very protective manager – I'll call him Noel – who took a keen interest in his staff's health and welfare. Employees were kindly reproached for overdoing it, and were too often asked if they were all right. When they replied "Yes", they were asked again, "Are you sure now? You don't look well." I sometimes thought Noel wanted them to be ill so he could look after them.

Noel ran around in a flap doing things he should have delegated. Why did he do this? He answered, "Well, I don't like to give them any more to do, really. I mean, it's not right, is it? They've got enough on their plates."

Not right? Noel's team was the laziest bunch of employees I had seen in a long time. One of them openly filed her nails at her desk and made long, loud and tedious calls to friends in work time. Lunch breaks were very long indeed, and the fetching of tea and coffee seemed to go on all day. Cakes were frequent, and cards, decorations and ornaments seemed to overwhelm the office. But Noel spoke to them all as if they were delightful children in a tone of voice best reserved for getting a two year old to eat their dinner. He often took over work they hadn't finished to make sure they got away on time, and slowly worked his way to a breakdown. The most effective employees, irritated by being stifled, had left long ago. Noel was left with the ones who had discovered a great little holiday camp.

Behavior has a habit of breeding behavior. If people are treated like children they often start to act like children. Certainly some of them will complain, "He talks to me as if I'm a child." People can start to play games. They may behave in naughty ways that baffle the manager who cannot understand what's happening.

For managers who protect their staff from taking on responsibility, there can be a slow realization that employees are "leaving everything to me, not finishing things and assuming I'll fix everything for them." The problem is circular. Noel realized that he'd made a mess of it but he was conflicted. He had worked for many years for a boss who was just like Stan.

"I always said to myself, after listening to my old boss belittling people day in and day out, that if I was ever a manager, I would never treat people that way," he told me. Noel was a polite and gentle man. Unfortunately, he had gone to a fatherly extreme at work and was killing the effort (and nearly himself) with kindness.

Every boss has to learn to speak to their employees as respected equal colleagues, no matter what task they perform. And that can be a struggle – particularly if, deep down, you don't have respect, or you have very fixed ideas about how people at work should be spoken to. Frankly, you'll find all of this advice a bit tough if you're wedded to the notion of class, and you've been raised to think that some people are elevated in society and should be kowtowed to, while others are lower and need to be reminded of their place. You'll also struggle if you're like Noel, and worry a great deal about being liked and loved. (Stan worried about control and being right all the time.)

Talking across to others – adult to adult

Barking at people or abusing them, like Stan, are not sustainable options, but turning passive or becoming a doormat like Noel, isn't effective either. The only viable professional option is to talk to people assertively in an adult-to-adult tone with the matching behaviors and word choices.

What does adult or assertive communication look and sound like?

To achieve an adult or assertive style of communicating, your voice should be steady – professional and reassuring but fairly unemotional. The conversations should be focused on looking for a solution in order to move forward rather than looking for someone to blame. In adult conversations, other people open up to ideas and challenges, and tend to come back with questions or their own ideas. Adult communication and active listening go together. Body language is easy and relaxed.

Assertive, adult communicators talk to people as if they are equals – because they are equals. A lot of the petty issues that can infest a workplace are greatly reduced. It makes work a more enjoyable, respectful place when people talk to each other as peers.

In short, if I'm treated as an adult I'm more likely to behave as one, and take responsibility for the work. It's likely I'll start to care more about the quality of the work, the customer at the end of it, and the colleagues who rely on me. When I am treated as a partner it's highly likely I'll behave as one.

Why we can struggle to be assertive

Just as some bosses can bristle at the notion of praise or listening actively, I've heard some very common objections to the idea of talking to employees as equals at work.

1. Isn't it quicker to shout?

It certainly feels quicker. Sometimes it feels good to let out a blast of anger, so we feel sure it must also be effective. But if you have a communication problem with someone and you shout at them, then you've just made it worse. It's only going to take you longer to get things back to a professional level.

2. I'll keep aggression up my sleeve for when it's necessary.

See above. It will only make things worse.

> *He that complies against his will is of his own opinion still.*
> *Samuel Butler*

3. Using first names is disrespectful.

Stan labeled anyone who used his name as a "cheeky bastard". If someone is old enough to earn a living, pay taxes, vote, marry, and drive a car, then why would you treat them as if they're still at school and you're the headmaster?

4. *Surely managers are also superiors?*

I recall a manager who made everyone stand in front of her desk when they went to speak to her. Because she was fairly short, she would remain seated on a pile of pillows. Clearly uncomfortable at seeing anyone on an informal basis, she rushed behind her desk if you caught her off-guard. For a ten-second question she would insist that you make an appointment. There were many other little habits she had adopted to protect her belief that, as a manager, she should be spoken up to. Like Stan, she was the subject of various pranks, and stealing the pillows became a game among staff.

We all have different skills, abilities and wage packets. Of course we have lines of reporting, but no one is actually higher up or lower down than anyone else. The idea of talking to everyone as an equal is not easy for someone who's insecure and believes that the role of manager has genuinely elevated them over others. If you truly believe that the people reporting to you are *less* than you, then this will affect the words you choose, your tone of voice and your body language when you're communicating at work. And you will never be a decent manager.

5. *I work in a tough environment.*

Many of us are taught that being heard means shouting the loudest and letting everyone know who is boss. We've been wrongly informed that being tough equals being aggressive or even abusive, and that talking respectfully to someone weakens us in some way.

Talking to people adult to adult is not a soft option. It is the choice of a professional.

6. *Some people have just got to be spoken to that way. It's the only way to get through to them.*

I often hear this kind of comment from managers, who are simultaneously complaining about low morale and belligerent employees. It's a lesson for many that we can only achieve difficult things by winning cooperation from other people.

You can remain calm and professional and still execute the less pleasant tasks a manager must perform, like giving a warning, firing someone or delivering bad news. In fact, staying calm is the *only* effective way to do these things. How exactly would shouting and talking down to people help the situation?

7. *They won't respect me unless I show them who's boss.*

The manager who is stuck in the habit of talking down to their employees may worry that he or she may be letting go of control by talking to others as equals. This is far from true. (Although Stan's team did wonder if he was up to something on the rare occasions he tried to do something about his behavior.) You can only *earn* respect. You start earning it by showing others that you are, at the very least, in control of your own behavior. You make the wise choice in dealing with people if you approach everyone with common courtesy and tact.

Power is an odd thing. It seems that the more you give it away the more you gain back.

8. *Isn't that all a bit too chummy?*

Talking as equals and colleagues is not the same as talking as mates. Being adult and assertive doesn't mean I am everyone's buddy either. It is a fairly neutral style of behavior.

9. *Sometimes I just lose it. I get tired or annoyed.*

Everyone gets tired and annoyed. It's only human. We all feel tested. It becomes difficult to stay in that professional adult style when the other person does not reciprocate, or provokes you in some way. We can be shaken when we're spoken to aggressively, or when we're antagonized by whining or unhelpful obstruction. But once again, if you lose it you have only gone backwards. Now you just have more work to do to get back to a professional level of communication and sort out the problem.

There's also great satisfaction in not allowing the other person to dictate your reactions.

FIVE THINGS EVERY MANAGER CAN DO TO IMPROVE THE WAY THEY COMMUNICATE

1. *Do some genuine reflection on the tone of your voice and body language.*

> *An eye can threaten like a loaded and leveled gun, or it can insult like hissing or kicking: or, in its altered mood, by beams of kindness, it can make the heart dance for joy.*
>
> *Ralph Waldo Emerson*

Emerson warns of only one aspect of body language that can impact the message received: eye contact. But your voice – its speed, pitch, volume, accent, modulation and, very importantly, tone – helps or hinders any message you are trying to convey. Your posture, dress, facial gestures, hand gestures, and any number of physical cues can also support or undo any situation you may be in.

There is plenty of room for misunderstanding, so try to make sure the message is lined up with the voice and body language. If your actions and tone are inconsistent with your words, people will look at the actions. You know the reason why – actions speak louder than words.

For example, if you tell people they've done a great job but you walk past too quickly and mutter it, do you think they'll believe you?

It's a great idea to get some constructive feedback about your body language from someone you trust and respect. It will be worth it if you're prepared to take note and make some improvements.

2. Get comfortable with differences in perception.

People read and hear things in their own way. Most bosses at some time will have scratched their head in wonder that such a simple message got so twisted around. In a crowd of a hundred listeners there can be more than a hundred interpretations.

We have to learn to live with differences in perception. You can do things to reduce the chances of misunderstandings but you'll never completely eliminate the risks. Be careful with what you write and what you say. Focus on the key facts, and accept that it's your responsibility to make sure you are understood. You're never going to deliver one hundred percent clarity, but if you establish a habit of being approachable – where people are free to come back and say "I'm sorry I didn't understand" or "I'm still confused, can you explain that again" – then your communications have a better chance of being understood as you intended.

3. Try to be more proactive.

The word "proactive" means to make things happen or to be on the front foot. This is opposed to being *re*active – waiting for things to happen or responding when you absolutely have to respond. And both are a far cry from operating in a bubble and always wondering what the hell happened.

Proactive bosses go out of their way to talk to people, to ask them how they're doing, to introduce themselves to everyone, and to generally try to make it easier for people to feel comfortable approaching the boss. This is all made easier if they know your name and if they've spoken to you in a relaxed manner before.

However, if you wait for people to come to you then you will miss out on too much.

Reactive bosses might insist that "my door is always open" but this is a pointless phrase if the overall message is "You come to me." And many reactive bosses will insist that they know exactly how the business is going because "if people had a problem, they'd come and tell me about it."

This is especially important advice for shyer managers and bosses. You're not alone in feeling hesitant about walking up to people and starting conversations, but you must get into the habit of it. It does get easier. If you're not sure how to start, then just walk up to someone with your hand stretched out and say "I'm sorry, I don't think we've met. I'm Hubert Pumpernickel. How are you?" In normal circumstances, the person will respond.

If you can't think of much to say, then ask people about themselves. Not as an interrogation, but just say something like "How are things with you?" People like talking about their kids if they have them. They usually have interests and hobbies. It doesn't take long to find something that people like to talk about. In one way or another, we like talking about ourselves.

Dale Carnegie wrote a wonderful book about interpersonal skills called *How to Win Friends and Influence People*. He suggested "Talk to someone about themselves and they'll listen for hours." Watch an expert communicator work a room or social situation and how they invariably make the other person the center of their attention.

4. Use open and probing questions more often.

This leads on from the point above. You listen and pick up on what a person is saying and ask for more information. If you want people to open up to you, then ask an open question. An open question is one that requires more than a one-word answer. Open questions get people talking. Questions that start with Tell me about … What do you think about … and Can you tell me why … (for example) open up conversations.

A probing question is one that follows up the answer they just gave you. Probing questions ask for more information. People don't always tell you enough or give perfectly crafted answers. If you want to know more, then you need to dig a bit. So are you saying … Does that mean … or, Why do you think that happened? are probing phrases.

If you just need facts and "yes or no" answers, or you're faced with someone who will not stop talking, then by all means ask some closed questions. These questions generally ask for one-word or very defined answers. Never ask closed questions when you're trying to find out the truth or get people to open up to you. They have a very halting effect and can be frustrating.

Good communicators are usually skilled questioners. They know that it's the person asking the questions who is steering the conversation.

Unless you start sounding like an FBI agent with an accusing tone, then most people will like being asked questions and enjoy sharing their point of view. We usually feel respected by the open question. If employees are not used to being encouraged to talk in this way then it can take a while for them to trust open questions. People can even be suspicious and very guarded, wondering what's going on perhaps, but they soon get used to it, and it forms an essential aspect of adult-to-adult communication.

5. Earn respect.

Influence is about pulling people toward you rather than pushing them where you want them to be. If you have influence, then people listen to you and are inclined to follow you because they choose to. If you search for communication techniques that help you trick, trap or corner people, or if you're hell-bent on copying some aggressive barking style straight out of a movie, then you're going to fail as a good communicator and therefore as a decent boss.

Aggression tends to corner people and they resent it. They resent it so much they may pay back the aggressor by tuning them out. Shouting makes people all the more anxious to defend what they already think. The worst strategy for an influencer is to be the one to shout loudest. One of the hardest lessons in influencing is that we do not win arguments if we intimidate the other person.

Trying to charm and manipulate your way is not wise. It will be seen through. As Abraham Lincoln said, "you cannot fool all the people all the time." Manipulative jargon laden with creepiness doesn't go down well. This is especially true if you're not perceived as having integrity. We get very cynical about managers who say one thing and do another.

Talk to people as equals.

Speak calmly, steadily and politely.

And always do this in difficult and unpleasant situations.

HANDLING UNPLEASANT CONVERSATIONS

There are times when you have to talk to an employee or group and you'd do just about anything to get out of it. Every boss has to have awkward conversations – giving necessary but embarrassing feedback, telling a group some bad news, rejecting a request. Sometimes managers have to provide instant counseling because an employee is suddenly in distress; that's not a natural skill for most of us. And at any moment a boss can be provoked, which is hard to handle, especially when it seems to come out of nowhere. These situations are a test for all bosses at any level, from lead hand to CEO.

There are some bosses who will avoid the situation, run from it, delegate it, or try to downplay the obvious need for the "unpleasant conversation". That's not going to work. More damage is done by delays and delegation.

Some managers will have the awkward talk, but be so vague that the employee or team is left wondering what it was all about, and may fill in the gaps with speculation.

The key is to be firm and fair and remember that managing people is not a popularity contest. People generally respect a direct approach and honesty. A fair bet is that someone would rather know than not know. Think about how you would like to be treated. You may be disappointed by bad news or upset by something unpleasant, but you'd feel even worse being kept in the dark.

Giving difficult feedback to one person

I was once asked to give some very awkward feedback to a young employee who was considered to be technically brilliant at his work. His manager felt that although he deserved promotion, he could not make the guy a supervisor because there were a few issues standing in the way.

Among these issues was the habit of wearing the same smelly shirt every day, complete with yellow stained armpits. He regularly forgot to do up his fly. He ate his lunch as if the canteen table was a trough and spat his food everywhere while talking excitedly about his work. His clothes and shoes were falling to bits. He clearly didn't visit a hairdresser or use shampoo. Let me add, this guy was extremely intelligent and earned a very good salary. He was also quite sweet and it was sad to see these things standing in the way of his success.

You may think it's shallow to hold someone back because of their appearance and personal habits, but businesses usually have to deal with customers or clients and they do need people who are presentable. Respect and confidence need to be earned, and we are imperfect creatures who make judgments about people. This smart young man was being talked about for the wrong reasons.

The manager asked me to give the feedback because he said he'd rather stick forks in his eyes. He didn't want to be seen as the bad guy.

I did it reluctantly. I think a manager's position is weakened by delegating conversations like this. The first thing the guy asked me was "Why didn't he tell me himself?"

No one wants to have conversations like these, but the manager did not understand the difference between being cruel and giving an employee the feedback that might help them to achieve their goals. Feedback of this nature is given with the intention of helping. If you keep that firmly in your mind, it will help you stay focused and constructive. It helps you get the tone of voice right. You're trying to build the person up rather than knock them down.

As it turned out, the guy in question *did* want promotion and he took the suggestions really well. The turnaround wasn't exactly rapid, and a bit of coaching was needed, but it was good enough.

So some useful tactics are:

1. Focus on what they need to do instead and be very clear in explaining that.

This can be as specific as asking someone to keep their voice down, stop telling filthy jokes that everyone can hear, wear some deodorant, chew with their mouth closed, or leave the inappropriate clothing for out of the workplace. I have had to have all of these conversations with employees.

Do say what you expect instead, and provide helpful solutions. If you say "You need to change your shirt each day" then you might also have to add "for a clean one." If you have to say "your breath is causing a problem" then you might have to give some advice on a solution, such as mints or keeping a spare toothbrush in an office drawer. If kicking off their smelly shoes in meetings is the problem, then you'll have to say so and then talk about keeping the shoes on or using some kind of foot deodorant.

Don't be subtle with these kinds of problems. Other employees have probably been joking around them and making sarcastic remarks for years without effect. And you cannot assume the person should know the solution. If they knew what to do, they'd be doing it. Direct is best.

2. Remind them that they are valued employees.

You can include some praise for the things they do well. You don't want them to stop the good stuff.

3. Tell them what you don't mean.

For example, "I don't mean that you need to buy an Armani suit, but what would help is if you dressed a bit more like Tom does."

4. Make this your observation and a private conversation.

This conversation is between two people. Talk about these delicate issues on a one-to-one basis. Do not say "the assistants have been fainting and the whole office came to me with a signed petition" even if that's true. Say "I have noticed" and "I think." Show some leadership here because this feedback could come as a shock.

If you say "I've had complaints" then it's very tempting for the person to wonder who complained about them. It could make them feel terribly self-conscious and isolated and that's not a good feeling for anyone.

In my experience, the person is almost always grateful if you handle this in a dignified way. They are often pleased to be told, despite the embarrassment. Occasionally there may be defensiveness or denial, but that's not typical if the conversation is handled properly. What can surprise you is when the person apologizes to you for your discomfort.

5. Use a kinder tone of voice than normal.

You should not deliver this kind of feedback in the voice of an army officer, but try not to sound like their fairy grandmother either. If in doubt, adult-to-adult, assertive tones work best. Think about how you would like to hear this.

We can put these particular conversations off forever and wring our hands for years hoping someone else will tell them. Talk to the person and do it in a timely fashion. This is one of those times when you earn your extra pay as a manager.

Giving bad news to a group

This advice is more geared towards those who work in larger businesses, but all kinds of bosses can find themselves in front of a group with some bad news. That group might not be employees; it might be customers or members of the public.

When bad news has to be announced it is not unrealistic to fear the mob's anger. If the group is large and it's very bad news, then you are exposed, and since we tend to fear public speaking at any time, it's not surprising that we might have genuine concerns about walking into such a situation.

I have seen managers calm down a volatile situation, and I have seen a group become angry through the insensitivity of a poorly handled bad-news briefing.

Before you start, do you know someone who has been in this position before? Talk over your worries with a manager whose advice you respect. And think carefully about how you would like to be told this if it was you on the other side of the conversation.

Can you break up people into smaller groups? It will take more time but it is more controllable and has a more personal touch than a giant town hall gathering. It's also easier for people to ask questions.

There's not going to be a perfect time to do this. When you're explaining some impending economic gloom or announcing some very unwelcome change, consider that the delay in waiting to hear is almost always stressful. If the company is in trouble, the rumor mill will already be working overtime. The smarter thing to do is clarify the situation as quickly as possible.

Never trick people by telling them they are meeting for some other reason. You only need to call everyone together for an announcement or a management briefing. I recently heard of a large company calling hundreds of people together for a safety talk, when in fact, they were announcing to all those gathered that they had lost their jobs. This was cowardly and ill-advised, and was done by a company with vast PR, HR and Communications resources to come up with a better way to do this. And just think about the impact of that tactic on the future efforts of the safety people.

1. Be brief, be clear and move on.

Don't dress it up. Obviously do this in person. Hiding behind a memo, noticeboard or text message (in the case of one British company letting their staff go) is also cowardly.

2. Remember that this is not about you.

Don't tell the group hearing the bad news how much you agonized over telling them, and how you haven't slept and how your ulcer is playing up, because it just prompts reactions like, "Well how the hell do you think we feel?"

If you want to say "I know this is disappointing" or "I wish this didn't have to be the case" then it's OK to say so, but don't make a long speech about your feelings because no one really wants to know.

If you're letting people go, don't say, "This is as hard for me as it is for you." It isn't. You're not going home unemployed. Not yet anyway.

3. Manage questions.

Being in question sessions at bad-news briefings can be like watching sharks circling. Once someone draws blood, a feeding frenzy can start. Some people do not seem to know the difference between a question and a speech.

Say up front that you're happy to take any questions at the end but that some may be best handled off-line if they are personal. But don't make an announcement and walk away without an opportunity for any questions at all. If you can't answer a question or you don't feel adequately briefed or prepared, then say so and come back with an answer at a later time.

4. Try a bit of empathy.

You don't know what other problems are going on in people's lives. There's no need to adopt a tone that is defensive or aggressive. If the people involved have not personally caused this problem or contributed to it, why speak in a way that gets their backs up? You can be a little kinder in your tone and show a bit of understanding.

5. Promise to follow up.

Do not leave everyone hanging. Make a commitment to come back with more information at an appropriate time and day. You could also commit to coming back as soon as you know anything further.

6. People are egocentric. They want to know how this affects them personally.

Remember that everyone standing there is thinking "What's going to happen to me?" You need to be as honest as possible. Sometimes people want promises and guarantees that no one can give. You cannot see five years into the future. You might need to say that. If you think that some really hard times are ahead for the business and that cash will be very tight, then maybe you should tell them that. Explain any help that will be provided if things are already sliding. If there is anything they can do to help, tell them that too. Good managers can get people to pull together in crisis and come up with solutions that can help the business survive.

No one is going to tap dance out of a bad news meeting. There are ups and downs to managing, and these occasions are definitely on the down list. I don't think you can ever learn tips that would allow you to be unmoved by these situations. Heaven help you if you did.

Saying no or rejecting someone

Every boss has to say no.

No, you can't go ahead with that.

No, you can't go on leave right now.

No, you didn't get the promotion.

No, I'm not renewing the contract.

Every time you make a decision, you're saying yes to one option and no to another.

For the same reasons that we would rather not give painful feedback or announce bad news, we can put off saying no. This is partly because we think we're rejecting the person. But we're not – we're rejecting a request or an option.

Put yourself in the shoes of the person who is waiting to hear a yes or no. Waiting is awful. Knowing allows us to move on. People waiting for a decision know that there is a risk of rejection. They have already gone there in their mind.

If you wish you could say yes then there's no harm in saying that. It's better to acknowledge some regret than sound unsympathetic or callous.

If you can explain why you've had to say no then do so. "We simply don't have the funds this year" or "We can't have two people on your grade on leave at the same time."

Sometimes people demand to know more about why they've been rejected than you're obliged to say. Do remember that you don't have to go on justifying your decision. You're entitled and empowered to make decisions, good ones and stinkers. Don't be backed into a corner. If push comes to shove, remember that "no" is a complete sentence, unless you have some new information that really does change the decision you just made.

For more on handling rejected job applicants, see the chapter "Finding People".

Handling a counseling situation

At some point every boss will have an employee talk to them about a personal problem.

As a boss you're going to hear private and personal things about employees and their lives, their health, their relationships, why they need time off, why they've been late or distracted, why they're upset or why they keep dropping boxes.

These situations need to be handled as confidentially as possible. Sometimes it can be helpful or necessary to share the person's situation with relevant employees so that some flexibility can be given and a bit of understanding shown.

You'll need those active listening skills again – to be quiet, ask open questions and show some support. Try to avoid taking on their feelings personally. Give them space and time to talk in private. Have the tissues handy.

If you work in a larger organization then there may be the option of referring the person to someone else if they wish, or calling in support. You might (carefully) suggest some community or medical support services that are appropriate and helpful.

Big companies tend to outsource counseling these days. Even so, those employee assistance programs only handle a fraction of the personal conversations that managers often face with maturity and good listening skills.

The need for you to be an instant counselor can come without warning. At least you can prepare a bit for the other three situations above, but you may find yourself suddenly facing a distressed, tearful, or just beaten down employee who asks "Have you got a minute?" and you have to focus your attention very quickly.

It's also very tricky when you do not like the person or do not feel moved by their situation.

Try very hard to resist giving personal advice.

The hardest thing for a manager in a counseling situation is to understand that you really should not give advice in these situations, even if the person asks "what would you do?"

Managers are asked for their opinion and advice all day. When someone brings us a personal problem, it can be very tempting to jump in, thinking *Hey, I know the answer to that and surely it will help them to hear it.* But the problem may be whether or not to end a relationship. This, along with many other personal quandaries, is not something you should decide for someone else.

When your job as a manager suddenly becomes that of a counselor, the challenge is to help the person think through their own problem. The task is not to think up an answer for them. What you can do is offer suggestions and alternatives carefully.

Statements such as "Well, he's obviously no good. I'd ditch him" or "Oh, tell her to stop worrying. I've had that test and it's nothing" or "Geez Louise! Your kids walk all over you, don't they?" are not very helpful. You might be tempted to make these kinds of comments but you really have to keep them to yourself.

However, good questions can be helpful. For example: What do you really want to do? How do you see that working out? What do you think would change this? You're helping them to think through their own personal problem. It's not your problem to solve – it's theirs.

Though it may throw you and feel like an unwelcome challenge, it is a good sign when someone seeks you out in the middle of a personal crisis. It's a mark of the esteem you're held in if an employee assumes they can tell you a private matter and that you'll listen and keep the conversation between yourselves. In short – you've done well.

Employees do not, in my experience, share personal problems with managers they describe as cold, psychotic, indifferent, arrogant or stupid. They don't even share their good news with those kinds of bosses. If you've been managing for a long time, and you have never been approached in this way, then you might want to consider how you're doing in the people skills department. I would suggest the story isn't a happy one.

Handling irritation, provocation and obstruction

Managers are only human, and that means you'll probably have people working for you that you can't abide. That in itself is not a problem but you can't let it show. You still have to talk and listen to everyone with professional courtesy. In the workplace, you can't avoid people. You're paid to persist in order to get things done.

I worked on a project where most people struggled to talk to a guy who was unusually miserable. We would avoid asking him "How are you doing?" because he would answer with solemn replies such as "Well, it's another day closer to death." He performed at his job, which was the main thing, but his endlessly bleak view of the world provoked people.

I've seen employees who could tolerate a wide variety of bad behavior, but wanted to leap out of the nearest window because the guy who loved talking about his model train set was walking toward them for a chat.

I recall one very obstructive assistant who had mastered the art of saying no, to the point where I wondered what she did all day. She sneered at every request, and I can still see her arms folded and her eyebrows raised as people asked her to do things that were part of her job. Normally calm employees became red-faced with rage dealing with this woman, especially since her smoke breaks were so frequent that her clothes smelled as if she were on fire. Eventually her manager sent her on an interpersonal skills training course, hoping that the penny might drop. (It never does, by the way. A training course cannot magically fix problems like these. There is no way around giving direct feedback.) She came back to work and announced to the team that the "course has taught me that I need to learn to say no. I've been too helpful and taking on far too much work." There was a loud collective thumping of heads on desks.

Rarely do people ever see themselves as difficult. If they knew there was a problem, they'd probably have done something about it by now.

So how do you deal with being provoked or baited?

Some conversations are full of baiting comments that can catch us if we're not wary and throw us into defensive mode. We may start having a separate argument that has nothing to do with the original subject matter.

There are at least four main baiting traps that I believe cause the most grief.

1. Irrelevant and tangential logic.

Question: Can you tell me why you're not wearing your safety glasses?
Answer: That bloke over there wasn't wearing his hard hat last week.

Question: Can you format the document this way?
Answer: We didn't do it like that at my last company.

Question: Why aren't you attending the course on the new system?
Answer: I've been in this business for twenty years.

These irrelevant sorts of responses can cause us to veer off into a different conversation. The reply sounds logical for a split second but it's got nothing to do with the request. It's like taking something faulty back to a store and being told "No one else has brought one of these back." Who cares? You are bringing one back.

"I've been in this business for twenty years" and similar remarks are a common blocking response. We're supposed to back away and be automatically respectful, but years served don't mean much unless the person adds some relevant and meaningful objection. On its own, what does it say? Don't you dare tell me anything? I'm beyond learning? That I know it all? That I've worked perfectly and progressed onwards and upwards for twenty years? You probably know people who have been driving for twenty years and still shouldn't be on the road. Without a valid argument attached to it, it's not much of a defense.

2. The history lesson.

If you're dealing with the present and the other person (or group) reaches back in time and says "Back in 1923" or "When Mrs. Jones was in charge" or "Thirty years ago, management told us ..." then you're in danger of fighting old arguments and getting sucked into unresolved issues. If someone is offering relevant and useful knowledge from the past, that's a different thing, but chucking in historical references without making a useful point, is a common blocking tactic and distracting ploy.

This can be woefully common in workplaces where people have never changed their job title or role in the business. Groups and teams can hijack meetings with an unplanned visit to the museum of the mind.

Side conversations such as "and do you remember when they had that awful business in the fifties?" are not a problem at the lunch table, but these history lessons can be a huge frustration when you're trying to get things done, bring in change and move a conversation along.

3. Argumentative bait.

When someone picks up petty detail or stages little fights that are not important, you can be trapped by a ploy designed to stall, sabotage, or just ignore you with argumentative bait. If you were presenting a report, for example, and someone said "I see on page 12, there's a comma missing in the second paragraph," then you have a good example of argumentative bait.

Argumentative bait can sound like this:

No you didn't.
Yes I did.
You said 200.
No I didn't, I said 150.
I distinctly recall it was 200.

Sometimes these details matter but often the nitpicking is designed to derail. When significant time and energy is taken up arguing the small stuff, the other person (or group) is usually doing their very best to avoid cooperating with you.

4. Manipulative bait.

Manipulative bait is the nastier, meaner commentary designed to insult and hurt your feelings.

When the responses are personally cruel, or intended to make you feel inadequate or guilty, then you are dealing with manipulative bait. Manipulative baiting can be directly insulting and provocative.

Here's an example of manipulative bait that resulted in a hefty payout to the highly qualified woman it was thrown at in a meeting. "Why aren't you home getting your husband's dinner ready?"

There are occasions when an employee wants endless stroking as to how wonderful they are, and exhibits frequent dummy spits in order to extract praise. "Well, if this happens again, I'm out of here." Most of us feel that there is some end limit to this kind of manipulative baiting.

Some other examples of manipulative baiting are:
Who the hell do you think you are?
What do you think you can tell me?
That's just typical of someone like you.

If you were more of a professional you'd make a different decision.

My last manager didn't care about that, but then he was a good bloke.

If you have a quick and wicked sense of humor and can come back with great zingers, then you may experience some sense of victory. It's also possible you'll later regret that you didn't stay cool under pressure. For the rest of us who can only think up a clever retort about twenty-four hours later, there is hope.

With all forms of baiting and provocation we need a strategy for staying calm and carrying on. Here are some general tips for most situations involving irritation, provocation and obstruction.

The key thing is not to be diverted, so don't bite, don't bite, don't bite! (Got it?)

Stick to the point you're trying to make and move the conversation forward. You can say "Getting back to the point" or "We're digressing" and keep moving.

You can offer to discuss their issue at another time. This not only looks professional but is likely to stop more unhelpful interruptions. "Phil, I'd be happy to discuss that issue with you later, but can we get back to XYZ?" Roll straight on with the relevant issue. Don't pause for a petty argument, insult or distraction.

You should deal with manipulative comments that cross a line, but it's probably better to do this in private and make it known that the behavior was inappropriate and unprofessional.

You might try a negative question that summarizes the state of play. By simply asking "Are you saying that you're not willing to discuss the proposal at all?" you are calmly noting their blocking behavior without making a fuss. This kind of question pulls people up when they're being unreasonably obstructive. They may realize they are coming close to disobeying a reasonable order or forgetting the overall objective of the team, and yet it's adult and assertive behavior on your part because you are handing them a choice.

In the same vein, "When would you like to have this conversation, because we're clearly not moving forward right now?" is a useful kind of question. Again it sounds respectful, the person is being given a choice, and yet it reminds the other party that this issue is not going away.

There is no script that you can pull out of a drawer to tell you exactly how to handle all these situations. I say this because a company once asked me to write some sample responses at the back of a training manual.

A better tactic is to ask mentors and people you trust how they would have handled these situations in a professional manner without letting bad behavior hold up the works.

Being able to have dignified conversations with a wide range of people is a litmus test for any boss.

CHAPTER FOUR

GETTING WORK DONE

Giving people meaningful work to do and making sure that work is done

WHAT CAN BE DELEGATED?
WHO CAN YOU DELEGATE TO?
HOW TO DELEGATE
WHY THE RELUCTANCE – SIXTEEN GREAT EXCUSES NOT TO DELEGATE
SHOULD YOU EVER DO THE TASK?
DELEGATING REAL WORK

*

Managing is getting work done through other people.

Delegating is another word for managing. You can't say that you're a good cook if you don't know how to boil an egg, and you can't say you're a competent manager if you don't know how to delegate. It's that basic.

And unless you plan to do everything yourself, you must become very comfortable with delegating because, as Virgil once noted – and millions since have discovered for themselves – "We cannot do all things." Delegating is an especially useful skill if you want to live to see retirement.

It's a smart move for any boss to have capable, independent and confident people working in their team and good delegating attracts and motivates such people because it gives them meaningful things to do.

If you're ambitious, you should also delegate to develop people because competent people will make you look good. They will tend to stick around for the investment that's being made in their future livelihoods.

WHAT CAN BE DELEGATED?

The short answer is – just about everything.

To determine the tasks that can be delegated, start by listing the very few things that cannot be passed on to others. Your list should be very short. When you make that list, imagine you'll be away for a month and completely out of reach.

These items are usually on the "not for delegation" list:

- Some signing authorities and certain financial responsibilities stay with you, although you can arrange for temporary authority or powers at certain times.
- Hiring and firing decisions for the people who report to you are yours, although you may want to involve others in the hiring process over time.

- Discussions about your staff stay with you. You should never delegate a performance review or a disciplinary conversation to a member of your team.
- There are possibly certain appearances at meetings that can't be delegated – or can they?
- The decision about what to delegate and the control of the overall work plan remains with you, otherwise you're abdicating – and that's very different from delegating.
- Blame can't be assigned out. The ultimate responsibility remains with you.

WHO CAN YOU DELEGATE TO?

A good boss is aware of an employee's strengths and general competence, or tries to understand this as soon as possible if they are suddenly inheriting employees they do not know.

A delegation plan simply requires a piece of paper or spreadsheet with all employee names down the side and all the key tasks or skills required in your team across the top. Or vice versa, it doesn't matter.

Take time to complete this with your own symbols or words after careful observation and perhaps consultation.

Now consider the following:

- Where is a team member fully competent at a task?
- Where is a person incompetent (at a task) at this point in time?
- Where is a team member gradually becoming competent? (What remains of the gap between what they can do now and what would make them fully competent?)
- Who could be helpful to train and coach others?

- In what areas will a person never be competent? For example, you may conclude that an employee will never be able to lift heavy items or operate certain machinery.

Make sure your reasoning is free of prejudice and that there is a genuine barrier.

You need to use your own observations, but perhaps incorporate the thoughts of other cool heads. Simply asking an individual about their competence is not wise. We tend to be quite poor at realizing our true strengths and weaknesses. Some will overestimate. Some will underestimate. Most of us are a bit blind to our real talents and shortcomings.

If the atmosphere is healthy, employees can be honest about what they can do easily and where they need support or training. You do need to use some sensitivity or word will spread pretty quickly that cutbacks are afoot. You may also find people asking to train up in some tasks. A smart employee wants extra skills and experiences to add to their resume and increase their prospects in the long term. You might also discover you are woefully exposed and dependent on too few people to perform certain tasks.

Think very carefully about someone's readiness to do a task. People are always at different stages of independence. Some want a bit of support but are reasonably comfortable in doing the task. Some want lots of support and are unsure about the task. Some need very little support or training and would make useful trainers or mentors. And some employees will know a hell of a lot more about the task than you do.

Confidence and competence can be fluid. An employee who was confident driving a car or truck may have lost their nerve. Perhaps the vehicle has changed. Perhaps they crashed their car and don't trust themselves behind the wheel right now.

A very able employee may be intimidated by, for example, suddenly having to work in an open office, or feeling out of step with new technology that changes their role significantly. Things may be happening at home that affect someone's ability to cope with changes at work.

Our needs for support and skill training shift about, usually developing in a positive direction, but not always. A good manager keeps their eye on people and remains approachable so that any employee can be honest about what they need.

Getting the balance right is one of those plate-spinning feats that managers have to learn. You don't want to tell someone how to suck eggs. You know how irritating it is when a backseat driver tells you how to drive. Your nostrils begin to flare and you can start to lose concentration. The irritation you feel makes it far more likely that you'll make a mistake.

But you don't want to leave someone alone with a task when they really don't know what to do or where to start. Not only does that threaten their confidence, but there could be a serious impact on health and safety, quality or service.

And don't leave independent performers entirely without support. Value these people who make your life a lot easier. They still want some recognition. Be careful they're not so underutilized or lacking in challenges that they're bored. Maybe they can help out with some of the coaching that you need to provide to other employees.

If you move around the workforce or through a large company, then you may find yourself managing people who are doing something you don't even understand, with strong qualifications and experience.

There may also be a future manager among your employees. This is where a boss needs some inner confidence and strength. You are the coach. What would any good coach do with a star player? Encourage and inspire this person to do well, or thwart them and show that you're insecure? You're being paid to coach now and not necessarily to kick the goals.

So once again, a plan that shows strengths, competence and readiness is a critical starting point project for delegation. The plan is now a basic training plan. It's just practical, and lightens the burden on your memory to have all this in some recorded shape or form. It's simply a part of leading, planning, organizing and controlling.

HOW TO DELEGATE

- Start with an overall plan of where your business (or your part of it) is going.
- Decide (with help if necessary) the meaningful work that will meet or exceed the plan.
- Decide who will do these tasks.
- Explain clearly the specific results that you want and the deadlines or milestones.
- Check the other person's understanding – what do they think you are asking for?
- Use some means of checking on the work that doesn't constitute looking over their shoulder all the time.

These basic steps apply whether it's a day shift or a five-year project.

Make sure that the person doing the delegated task knows that you want to hear about a genuine problem or difficulty, should one arise. You don't want to be told on the day the work is due "I couldn't do it."

Never make delegation decisions based on the appearance or general noise made by the busy brigade. Look carefully – it might be a performance. When you take claims of busyness at face value and shift workloads accordingly, you can accidentally reward panic merchants and encourage all their inefficiencies, and punish quiet achievers who are effective workers.

Larger projects and assignments should be challenging but within reach. Impossible targets are demoralizing and can have some consequences in health, safety and quality.

Make sure employees are comfortable asking constructive questions about what they've been asked to do. Learn to separate the "I don't see why I should have to" phrase, from the "I'm not sure why we do it like that. Wouldn't it be better if …?" kind of contribution. Your business needs people who can find sensible shortcuts and identify wasted effort, spot potential problems and find better systems.

DELEGATE AS AN ONGOING PROCESS

Delegation is not something you do as an occasional project. It's not a handy trick that you learn at the end of a time management course to pull out of the hat when you're busy. It is the ongoing process of managing people and tasks.

Record the work you have delegated and the timelines. Use a spreadsheet, diary, wall chart, whiteboard, the latest gadget or an exercise book – it doesn't really matter. There's no right way to practice delegation or time management, although writing on the back of your hand is not ideal, and yellow sticky notes can be lost in a sudden breeze. Use a system that works for you so that you know, and can quickly view, who is doing what. Those records are going to be extremely useful when you come to review performance and make other decisions relating to your employees.

If you don't follow up on a delegated task, you'll send a message that the work didn't matter. Eventually, a general failure to follow up will result in people either neglecting the tasks you give them completely, or deciding that it's not worth doing a good job on them. There could be a direct impact on health, safety and quality when employees decide that the task doesn't matter. Wouldn't you come to the same conclusion if no one seemed to notice the task you had finished? How long would it take you to lose the desire to do it well?

WHY THE RELUCTANCE TO DELEGATE?

Here are some very honest comments made by managers I've known on the subject of delegation.

"I've always struggled with delegating. Something has to be done properly, but at the same time I know the person has to develop. It's so tempting to pick it up and just do it yourself, but I know this is a destroyer of confidence and that in the long term I'll just create more work for myself. I also know from my own experience how much I hate it when a boss does that to me, and it's the kind of irritating thing that makes you start looking for work elsewhere." (Ella, lawyer)

"I felt so worried about the responsibility I'd been given that I thought I couldn't let anything go wrong. Not only did I fail to plan and organize and all of that stuff, but I kept trying to do my old job. Then I started picking up all kinds of crap from people, tasks I knew the old boss hadn't done for them. They were delegating upwards. Some noticed my fear and insecurity and probably thought, 'Well if you're so worried about it – do it yourself.' I couldn't let my old work go. I figured they'd promoted me because I'd done so well with it, what would happen if I let it fall in a hole?" (Martin, engineer)

"I was managing people who were much older than me and I felt embarrassed asking them to do things. One of the women used to give me this 'oh yeah' sort of look and I was nervous asking her to do anything. I was afraid of her and she knew it. So I kept asking the people who seemed really cooperative and eventually I overloaded them. They got angry and I understood why. The lady with the 'oh yeah' sneer was clearly testing me, wanting some sort of confrontation, and she was stirring up the people who started questioning whether I was overloading them. I got into a mess and I had absolutely no idea how to get out of it." (Louise, payroll manager)

We can all get into a mess with delegation. New bosses are frequently thrown in at the deep end without training and support about what the role of the manager is, and what it isn't. But there are lots of reasons why we might fail to delegate, and some of these habits and attitudes can also stay with experienced bosses.

SIXTEEN GREAT EXCUSES FOR FAILING TO DELEGATE

1. *It's quicker to do it myself.*

It's much quicker if we spoon feed a toddler and so much tidier. At what age should our children still be wearing a bib and allowing us to feed them? It's nicer if we leave the training wheels on children's bikes and avoid the scabby kneecaps and tears. We'll certainly worry a whole lot less.

Again, at what point do we make a fool of them with those training wheels?

We all understand this example of a parent smothering their child and how absurd it would be to discourage independence in this way. But we can fail to see that we often spoon feed adult employees. Some managers take irrational steps to avoid the necessary pain and mess of gradual independence and growth.

Of course it's quicker if you do it. It's probably the reason you were promoted, but if you delegate and develop people, then fairly soon they'll do the task quickly too. Let them grow, or your best employees will go to another job to be treated as an adult.

> *Spoon feeding in the long run teaches us*
> *nothing but the shape of the spoon.*
>   E M Forster

2. I get whining or resistance when I ask someone to do something.

We've probably all observed the employee who sulks if asked to do anything. Shoulders and face drop as if you've asked them to help build a pyramid.

Some folk can become like toddlers and say no to everything, although these refusals at work can come out as "Why should I?", "Do I have to?", "Why pick on me?" or even a prolonged stare.

Observe people's capabilities and readiness to take on a task, but if you meet with some unusual resistance, challenge it. Be prepared to listen, but don't fall into playing a game.

Confidence can be a big issue. Skill may be an issue, but don't let a whine or a scowl put you off. Move on quickly and leave the task with the person you delegated it to. Belligerent people soon learn that you mean business and they might as well get on with it. Don't lose your temper or get distracted by churlish behavior. If someone has been getting away with shirking or delegating upwards for a while, then they're probably quite good at manipulating these situations. Don't fall for it.

3. They said they couldn't do it.

Is it a genuine training issue? If so, then training is called for. Is it about confidence or available time? Has there been a recruitment error?

If there seems to be no valid reason for saying no, then you could be facing something called "learned helplessness." It's easy to shrug and say "I can't do it" or "I don't really do that." Grown adults have been known to pretend that they can't iron a shirt, make a meal for themselves, wash dishes or wrap a Christmas present. I've known of an adult who pretended for years that he couldn't run a bath, and for years managed to find various people to run his bath for him.

I've pulled the old "learned helplessness" lever myself. When confronted by something I found unnecessary or boring, I've found ways to feign hopelessness so that some helpful person would do the task for me. This would include things like changing a tire or a printer cartridge. I still love people who step in and do these things for me. Who doesn't?

However, managers must challenge this behavior if they run into it, because people are paid to do work that is allocated to them. If they shrug and say "Can't do it" about some fundamental part of the job, then clearly something has to give, and it shouldn't be the goodwill of other employees or your time.

4. *They just said no.*

People rarely say no directly. They just don't do what you asked, or walk away, or shrug, or do something that indicates they are refusing the task.

But however it's expressed, you have to find out why they're refusing. Was it a dangerous task or an unnecessary one? Do they know how to do the task? Was it something outside their remit or competence? Did you ask? It's possible that they had a good reason for refusing. It's also possible you have a problem employee. See "Letting People Go."

5. *I feel embarrassed asking.*

Some managers worry about appearing bossy or say they feel awkward ordering people about. You have to get over that. Talk to people as equals and recognize that delegating work is the main thing that managers do. You're paid to manage workflow and you cannot possibly be producing all of it. When people come to work and report to you, they generally do understand you're supposed to be giving them work.

6. *I might look dispensable.*

You are dispensable.

As the former French Prime Minister Georges Clemenceau noted, "The cemeteries are full of indispensable men."

7. They're busy.

Some people will always say they're busy. A couch potato who watches TV all day can tell people that they're really busy. Don't be fooled by claims of busyness. That's not how you determine someone's effectiveness.

Is there a real need to look at workloads and a genuine need for overtime or more resources? Perhaps you do need reminding about other tasks and responsibilities that are pressing on an employee, but it's easy to be stonewalled too. You are a manager, and perfectly entitled to ask this question, "Tell me what else you've got on right now?"

Sometimes you'll discover people doing things that are no longer required, or to a level of perfection that is unnecessary. When killing off unnecessary tasks or perfectionism you can meet with resistance, but "We've always done it" is not a good enough response for a smart manager. Some perfectly valid questions are: Why is it necessary? How does it fit the plan? How does it create value? And if the explanations do not hold water, then you might have just found a good way to save time and money. That's great. Now there's some more time available for important work.

8. They might make a mistake.

Yes. They might.

We generally learn from mistakes.

If there's a security or safety issue, then delegation and training both need to proceed cautiously, but with a bit of planning, people do learn to perform a wide variety of dangerous tasks, like operating on other human beings, flying aircraft, swinging shipping containers about from cranes, minding small children, and using food processors with sharp blades, and they do these things without causing disasters (mostly) because their training has been thorough. Remember that someone gave you the chance to make mistakes when you were promoted and probably long before that day.

9. *They might not do it very well.*

No, they might not do it well the first or second time. Did you?

Have you got a training plan to help them improve? Are they being supervised until they learn? Will you give them feedback as they go?

10. *They might do it better than me.*

Watch out for your own feelings of insecurity. You are now paid to manage and not to keep proving that you are the best at the task.

11. *They might do it differently.*

This is highly likely. We're human beings and we think differently, and therefore approach tasks differently. What if their way turns out to be a better way? They might find a very acceptable shortcut that saves time and money. Is there a fixed and right way of doing this task? If not, remember that you need to see a result. How they get to it might not be terribly important.

12. I like that task and want to keep it to myself.

We can all get emotionally attached to an aspect of our job. If we did a task well, or built something, or ran a project with care, we can have trouble handing it all over to someone else. This is an understandable feeling. But here's a thought – if this task was fun and enjoyable to you then perhaps it will be enjoyable to others. Could it be delegated as a kind of reward? Perhaps the employee who deserves a boost would also enjoy this work.

If you're ambitious, remember it's harder for you to move onwards and upwards in your workplace if there's no one competent or confident enough to fill the role you left behind.

13. They're genuinely incompetent.

Have you had this person on the team for a while? Why are you keeping someone you believe is genuinely incompetent? Why are you paying someone to do a task they cannot do?

If they started recently, take a look at the way you recruit people. Get involved in the recruitment of employees if you're inclined to say "It's these people I get from HR."

The situation is not sustainable. Your good employees will start becoming very unhappy if you keep excusing incompetence with a lighter workload. And you're wasting resources, like time and money.

14. I like looking busy.

Do you like being a martyr? You're not alone. There are plenty of them. But looking busy is not what you're paid to do. Consider the example you're setting for everyone else.

You might be unwittingly creating a team of people who also think that looking busy and sounding exasperated is better than being effective.

15. It seems lazy.

You're not lazy because you delegate tasks – that's what you're paid to do. You're now paid to plan, lead, organize and control. If you're clearly doing those things, no one is going to say the boss is lazy.

16. If I delegate all my work, then what will I do?

Just a wild thought here, you could spend your day managing. Back to the previous point, you could excel at planning, leading, organizing and controlling. You can instigate and manage improvement projects. There will be more time to innovate, train and think. And if you're ambitious and have your eye on another job, then try to get some of that work delegated to you with all the free time up your sleeve.

SHOULD YOU EVER DO THE TASK?

There are circumstances in which you could find yourself doing rather than managing. However, if doing the task takes up a hundred percent of your time, then when are you managing?

Small business managers typically do a lot of tasks. You might also do a lot of task-work to help out in peak times, a crisis, a severe shortage of people, or just because you're keeping some manageable proportion of your time for the task itself. When first promoted to supervisor or lead hand it's typical that you would keep doing the task to some extent. In a training situation, you might still be the best trainer around.

You might also choose to hop in and do the task, in order to keep yourself aware of what's going on. It's a smart move for all managers to deal with customers when possible, and to understand first-hand what frontline employees are facing.

It should be mandatory for all managers in large companies to spend time at the place where the work is done, the product is sold or made, and the customers interact with the business. This can only help to reduce the problem of out-of-touch or ivory tower decisions being made.

DELEGATING REAL WORK

When you delegate work, it helps if you can explain how the task fits into the bigger plan. If the work has no connection to the plan, then why the hell is anyone doing it? Is there some legal reason for it? Is there some real benefit to the business?

Every single employee should be able to clearly understand how the work they do links to the greater picture. It's not their responsibility to make that connection. It's yours.

Do not delegate meaningless work. It can cause "rust out", which is as debilitating as burn out. If it's a wasted meeting, or form-filling for the sake of form-filling, then get rid of it. As a manager you need to be the chief gatekeeper on unnecessary activity. When looking for cost cuts, look at unnecessary work before you fret over other cost cutting.

You're in dire need of help if you're away from work and return to find your desk covered in paper and a hundred people needing to speak to you urgently. Your absence should not spell chaos or a standstill. I've seen managers trying to set this up, so that they appear to be indispensable while they're away.

Good managers are good delegators. Employees who work for smart delegators do not claim they're being taken advantage of. They tend to say they're learning a lot or getting somewhere. People who are busy doing meaningful work that they know will contribute to the purpose of the business generally say they like their work.

You should be proud of yourself if you come back from any meeting, conference, sick day, training course or holiday and find that everything is going fine. If the place is running well, it probably means that everyone knew what to do and got on with it. People knew who to ask for help, how to keep things going and they had plenty to do.

Only worry if no one seems to recognize you.

CHAPTER FIVE

FINDING PEOPLE

FINDING GOOD APPLICANTS
CONDUCTING INTERVIEWS
MAKING A DECISION
ONBOARDING OR INDUCTING NEW STARTERS

*

Few processes impact the success or failure of a business as much as the selection of the people who will work in it. And few bosses realize that new starters decide in their earliest days of employment how long they will stay.

Recruiting people is not a science. It's not about judging a beauty parade either. The aim is to make the best decision you possibly can for the future of your business while accepting that mistakes will be made. We can't make fabulously accurate predictions about people and we can't measure their potential or personality, but we can usually do a bit better at the way we recruit people and get them started.

It's common today to see large businesses treating the vital process of recruitment as something that can be handled by an e-system, or outsourced like the supply of stationery. Indifferent recruitment shows up quickly in areas like quality, customer service, morale, safety, and ultimately on the bottom line. It should never be treated with such indifference.

But recruitment can be daunting. One good friend, I'll call her Jane, runs her own business and says, "I just hate the whole recruitment thing. When people tell me they're leaving, I'm sure my face falls at the thought of going through all that again. I dread interviews. I don't know what I'm supposed to be asking. The worst part is that I never know who to pick. They all sound good at an interview. Their CVs all look good to me."

I'm writing this chapter with Jane in mind. She's like a lot of managers and is brilliant at many things, but dreads this side of being a good boss.

FINDING GOOD APPLICANTS

The first stage of good recruiting starts with seven steps, which sounds cumbersome, but they're all crucial.

Step 1: Decide what the business needs with a simple job specification, or "job spec".

Few people make a significant purchase without some careful thought. Most of us take our time before investing our hard-earned money. So a good boss does not take on an employee, at great expense and risk, without putting time and effort into the decision up front, because it's far easier to return a bad purchasing decision than it is to manage out an employee who is not right for the business.

The biggest mistake that most bosses make is underestimating the value that exists in good preparation and real thinking about a newly vacant role. Every time you have a vacancy you are handed the opportunity to look closely at that job and at your business. This is a moment to make a positive change. Consider what you need and don't need.

A general exception to this would be if you are employing a number of people with very similar duties, for example, call center staff, drivers or couriers, cabin crew or graduate auditors. Even these roles change over time and sought-after requirements are reviewed, but many vacancies are one-offs and no one else performs that exact role in the business.

If it's not reasonable to review the specs at this moment and if they're still fit for the purpose, then you could skip to Step 3.

Put aside all thoughts about age, sex, qualifications and experience, and just consider what the jobholder is required to do. Are they required to manage the front of house at your restaurant? Are they required to get a music magazine out on time once a week? Are they required to design a pipe to take water through a desert? What is it that this jobholder must do and achieve? This does not require you to write an essay – your answer might take up one sentence.

A clear job spec helps you avoid the familiar trap of trying to fit a person's image to a vacancy. For example, "Phil is leaving. Therefore we need to find another Phil." It also makes it so much easier to write a relevant specification and then a smarter advertisement that might open up the potential field a bit more. It will also help you craft good interview questions and arrive at a sound final decision.

Some questions to think through and if necessary, reconsider the vacancy.

- Has anything changed about this job since you last recruited someone?
- Has the equipment or technology changed?
- Are you recruiting again because people keep leaving too soon? Why are they leaving?
- Do jobholders consistently fail at this role? Why?
- Are you confident about the way you have organized the work?
- Is the job rewarded appropriately? For example, if someone is required to work miracles and you're paying minimum wage, then you're going to have high turnover in this role.
- Do you need a full-time person?
- Do you need someone year-round, or could it be more seasonal or contractual?
- Is there an opportunity to employ someone looking for flexible hours? That's a large and useful pool to tap into when recruiting and it includes people looking for school friendly hours, job sharers and part-timers, people caring for others and many wanting to semi-retire.

Step 2: Write a person specification or person spec.

You should now be clear about what the person is required to do and achieve, and the time commitment required. The next step is to be clear about the skills, attributes and experience a person would need to possess in order to do this job effectively. Your aim is to attract strong applicants who are a fit for the role.

What sort of education and training would be a minimum requirement? If the role requires a person who holds a fork lift driver's license or the proven experience in designing shopping malls, then it should be included on the person spec, but be careful about putting up qualification or skills hurdles when they aren't necessary.

For example, before you include a master's degree ask yourself if this is essential and why you think so. What do you think this qualification is bringing to your business, and are you certain you can't ask for those abilities in other ways?

What kind of experience would be useful to meet this person spec? Decide on the length and type of experience that would be useful to your business. Consider whether they actually need any. You might prefer to train them.

Does their experience have to match your kind of business exactly? What about work in other industries, countries or circumstances, which might have produced a very good applicant?

So be clear and sensible about the absolute priorities and minimum requirements. This will not only help you write your person spec and help decide where to advertise the role, but it will also help you sort out the responses when they come in. Don't delay this until after you've interviewed people or you may try to fit your favorite candidate into the role.

Another trap to avoid is looking for someone who cannot possibly exist. This does happen – sometimes managers ask for attributes that are conflicting, or they start making a wish list bordering on the absurd.

For example, I was once asked to find a person who would report to two managers. One demanded that the person be a malleable, young team assistant. In his opinion, a bright school-leaver would be ideal and his idea of salary matched that age group. He suggested we should go to the local high school and share the vacancy with a careers teacher. His colleague, however, kept demanding a graduate who had a finance qualification and showed signs of being able to lead the department one day. He wanted the role advertised in the professional pages. These are two very different person specs and it simply wasn't going to work.

Another manager asked me to find some new people with "a fire in their ass." I wondered how I'd test applicants for that attribute.

Pay rates are usually determined by how much the business can afford, comparable grades and responsibilities, the community you work in, the industry you operate in and sometimes by legislated rates set within awards. This is an ongoing challenge in recruitment, and the larger the business, the bigger the challenge. Managers have to stop and consider the comparisons between what is going to be offered, and what is being paid to existing staff. But don't be too mean if you want good candidates. Remember that money and benefits will be important when people decide whether to apply or not.

Watch out for your own discrimination and bias when writing a person spec. Aside from the obvious perils of looking for "someone just like Phil" and actually seeking the same sex, age and cultural background, we can also apply unconscious bias to all our recruitment and promotion decisions and end up in a very sorry state.

Never insist on age ranges, races, gender, religion, politics, or other irrelevant requirements that are clearly designed to exclude people. It's unlikely anyone would be stupid enough to write them in an advertisement these days, but I've had managers instruct me to exclude people. It's one of those unpleasant facts of corporate life that has improved over time but there is a long way to go.

It's absolutely fine to decide that at least two years related experience is required, but it's not OK to write "must be 25 or under." What is this age requirement based on? Is it a belief that only those under a certain age have energy or can learn? If you're seeking that elusive quality called maturity and asking for someone in an older age group, are you assuming that older people are always more self-controlled?

You can state that applicants need to be available for a 24/7 roster, or possess the legal right to work in your country. You can ask to see valid and current licenses and warn applicants that they will need to pass a police check, but don't risk legal action by discriminating without a good reason. The law rarely allows us a valid reason.

Insisting on high grades is another trap. What do grades mean? What is the link between a grade and the likelihood of someone performing well in the role you're filling? Qualities such as commitment, self-control, and other essential interpersonal skills may not show up in grades.

What does "smart" mean? People are smart in different ways. If psychologists struggle to come up with a consistent definition of intelligence then what chance do the rest of us have?

Once again, be careful about putting barriers in place that might knock out a good applicant. A lot of dropouts have done pretty well for themselves.

I was a slow learner. Nowadays they have

ADD and all these different syndromes, but when I was a kid, we didn't have any of that. It was just 'Mrs. Eastwood, your son is a little slow.' I'm striking a blow for C students everywhere.

Clint Eastwood

Step 3: Write the most important interview questions after writing the specs.

Write the questions now? Can this be right?

It's the best time to do it. Write a couple of crucial questions while the job and person specs are fresh in your mind. You'll find it much easier to come up with the really important and obvious questions.

Think of the challenges the role will present and how an applicant might solve those. Consider starting questions with phrases such as:

- Can you give me an example of an experience that involved ...?
- Tell me about an incident when ...
- Can you explain how you might handle ...?
- If someone came to you and asked ...?
- How do you normally deal with ...?
- Have you ever had to ...?
- How would you ensure ...?

This is called behavioral interviewing, and these kinds of questions force an applicant to give you an answer based on real experience.

For example, let's say the job is handling the front of

house for a restaurant. Behavioral questions might include: How have you handled aggressive customers who demanded certain tables? Have you ever been in situations where the kitchen had serious delays and the bookings backed up? How did you cope? It's not easy for people to bluff their way with these sorts of questions. The ease in the way an applicant answers, the logic and good sense they display, or don't display, will help you choose between interviewees.

Step 4: Decide where to look for the person or make sure the right person looks for you.

When I started recruiting we placed all the salaried vacancies in the Saturday edition of the state newspaper. We also received a lot of general applications from people hoping to be considered if something came up. Occasionally we used the staff noticeboard. In one part of the business, men lined up at a gate on certain days of the week to be chosen for a day's work. It was a company where surnames were repeated on the payroll, because people were able to find jobs for family members. I started recruiting in a recession and the piles of applications occasionally toppled over.

Life has changed a bit. Today, advertising on internet recruitment sites costs much less than one Saturday advertisement. Company websites now contain careers sections that advertise vacancies. If you're keen to work for a particular company you can set up email alerts to stay informed.

What hasn't changed is that managers still want good candidates to know about their vacancy and feel encouraged to apply. You can be swamped with inappropriate applications from internet job sites, but there are other avenues still available for use when searching.

- If the role is a specialist one, then consider the trade or professional bodies they might belong to.
- Do you already have files of people who want to come and work for you? It's so much easier to employ from those who have gone out of their way to tell you they want to work for you.
- Do you have a noticeboard or intranet within your business, or access to community employment noticeboards or services?
- Could you go to local colleges or trade schools and offer the role to a graduate or near graduate?
- Do you have useful government job finder services or reputable agencies where this person may have already registered?
- Do your existing employees know of someone looking for such a position?

Never limit yourself to friend and family recommendations. It has an upside as a reward for good service and it's a positive sign that people are reasonably proud of their workplace. But it can also breed a closed-shop environment, which is rarely good for business in the long run. It can also make life difficult if someone has to be dismissed and friends and family remain in the business.

Recruitment agencies can be very slapdash – eager to grab a placement fee, with little regard for fit on the employee or employer's side. Some agencies are run like a used car yard. And be very wary of headhunters. Some are professional and do a sound search for a suitable candidate. And some, I'm afraid, do little more than ring to find people with the same title in another company. They may have no idea whether that person is a good performer because they don't check, and they have no authority to properly check in any case.

And of course watch out for the old saying "self-praise is no recommendation." Do not use social media to search for people because the invention of titles and experience on some of these sites is laughably wide of the truth.

Step 5: Write the job advertisement.

There are a lot of managers who will start the recruitment process by pulling out the last advertisement for the vacancy and tinkering with the details.

Your advertisement should include some basic information.

- Who is the employer and what is their business, in brief?
- Where is the job located? That will be one of the most important details for jobseekers.
- What is the title?
- What will this person basically do? This must align with the job spec.
- Who should the applicant contact for further information? Please don't hide behind e-recruitment systems. Provide a name and a contact number.
- How do you want people to apply? Should they phone first for an application form or send in a CV? If you force everyone to fill out online applications and refuse to deal with anyone on a personal level, then just be aware you may have lost a good candidate. There are sound reasons why some individuals would rather not leave their personal details on a recruitment site that cannot be secured.
- When do applications close?

- What is the salary range and are there benefits in addition to salary? At least be prepared to give out that information to interested applicants, even if you don't want to disclose all the specifics in the advertisement.
- Alert candidates to any travel requirements, shift work and weekend availability, working in all weather, and changes to work patterns at short notice. Consider anything related to the job that a person would need to handle and be comfortable with.

If you write a job advertisement that is clear then people will read it and know very quickly whether they fit the criteria or not.

Write about the role and your business in a positive light. Other people will be reading this too. And don't be afraid to use the plainest language. I love reading job advertisements that are really straightforward.

I also read some ads and wonder who could possibly fit the bill. For example, asking for applicants to have demonstrated gravitas makes me laugh out loud. I've also seen "You will have a master's degree, exceptional international experience and a track record for achievement. You will be in your late 20s."

I've seen an advertisement that asked for a casual warehouse operative to have a forklift license. No problem with that, but it went on to ask for a qualification in warehousing and distribution technologies. Why? Wouldn't that requirement be applied to the warehouse manager role?

And recently a large and wealthy property company advertised for a mailroom clerk. *Great*, I thought, *someone still has entry-level jobs for school-leavers and others needing a start*. Then I read further that they wanted applicants to have been experienced mailroom clerks elsewhere first.

Step 6: Handle and cull inquiries and applications.

Make sure you're organized to collect the applications as they come in. Get a file of some kind started and treat every inquiry with respect. You might acknowledge applications at this point. It's the polite thing to do. An applicant appreciates knowing their information landed in the right place.

Don't let other employees such as reception staff be anything other than polite to all who express an interest. It is not their role to deter people or share information indiscreetly.

You are likely to get people you know, such as existing employees, asking if you would consider them or someone they know, possibly a close relative. Don't dismiss them without a chance but insist that they must go through the same process as everyone else. Never respond with comments like "Your Darren? Do you think he'll manage to get off the sofa each day?"

Internal applicants should be welcomed and encouraged. They should always be interviewed, even if they're not suitable. When an employee puts their hand up to progress within a company then respond to that request with respect. This is a moment of truth where their motivation can be maintained even if they don't get the job. It's also a good opportunity to talk about their future and help them plan to close that gap between where they are and where they want to be.

When you reach the cut-off date for applications you can start to cull. Your aim now is to make the best match of candidate with your superbly sensible job and person specifications.

Separate out those who fit the basic requirements from those who clearly don't. At the first sorting, a Yes and No pile will do. Look again at the No pile and be certain. Is there anyone there of interest for something in future? Is there someone of interest to another part of the business?

What if you have no decent applicants at all? Something is wrong with your job spec, person spec or advertising choice. Go back to find out. You may have to start over.

Recruitment is a process of rejection, although we mistakenly call it one of selection.

Decent managers and smart human resources people reject applicants carefully. This is a time to be very conscious of prejudice. You're making this selection against criteria you set down earlier and thought carefully about, so it must not become personal. Try very hard not to let your biases run riot. So you have an application from someone who went to a particular school and those kids used to chase you down the street. It's time to put that nightmare aside.

Sift down your Yes pile and choose those who are a very strong match for your criteria. Preference should be given to those who might bring something extra with them – experience, or a skill your business could benefit from. Is there someone in that pile who stands out?

If you need further information from your close matches then ask for it now over the phone or email.

How many applicants you choose to interview is up to you, but as a general rule, don't waste other people's time. Don't interview someone just to fill a number in your mind. If you only have two suitable candidates then do two interviews. If ten are very close then interview ten.

Write a polite letter or email to those you are rejecting outright and thank them sincerely for their interest in the position and in your business. If you think you'd want to hear from some of them in future then let them know that. You may think this sounds old-fashioned. It's not. It's about maintaining a standard of decency in our behavior toward other human beings. A job seeker is someone who has expressed an interest in working for you and they have gone to some effort to ask for your consideration. One of the most frequent comments coming from the army of dispirited job seekers today is the lack of any response or feedback from potential employers. In my old-fashioned view, it is simply bad manners to leave people without any answer and, if you want to do a very easy thing to alleviate some pain in the world, send a reply.

If you asked for original certificates and photos then you must return them.

Step 7: Plan the interviews

When you're planning interviews you're caught between several needs. One is to get a good look at the candidate. As we can't read minds and do not possess the power to predict someone's future behavior, this is an optimistic exercise. Another need is that of effective selling. Recruitment is also a sales exercise because you want the best candidate to come to work for you and they might be lining up other offers. You're selling your business as a good place to join. You are selling yourself as a decent manager to work for, and the job as a meaningful thing to do each day. Strong candidates can afford to be choosy.

Interviewing is also a public relations exercise. You want everyone to go away with a positive image of your business, however big or small, because both they and their wide circle of contacts might be future customers. If they're angry at the way they were treated, it's likely you won't get their business and that your reputation will be tarnished in some way.

At one interview I had for a temp job the manager extended his hand for me to shake that was covered in machinery grease. He'd neglected to finish the cigarette that was stuck to his lower lip and offered me a mug of tea while swirling out a couple of mugs in a basin with a filthy wash cloth. His cigarette gave up a length of ash into one of the mugs and he didn't notice. The chair I was offered had to be cleared of porn magazines, spanners and someone's half-eaten sandwich. I didn't stay. In fact, I ran from the place.

Last but not least, interviewing people has legal ramifications because if you say or do something really stupid, you can land yourself or your company in hot water. Never make racist or sexist remarks, or ask irrelevant and intrusive questions about personal lives during an interview.

For example, do not ask about domestic arrangements, religious beliefs or relationships. You might think you need to know but you really don't.

Does the job involve a need to travel, work late or work weekends? If so, then state how often that would be likely and ask all candidates about whether they would be available.

That doesn't stop you asking some probing questions to individual candidates, but tread carefully. Go back over your shortlist and consider anything unique that you wish to follow up. For example, "I notice that you lived in Japan for two years. Can you tell us about working there?"

Practical steps to plan ahead of the interview:

- Set aside your diary time for the interviews. Space them to build in a buffer. Interviews often run longer than you think and you need time for notes and discussion.

- Notify the people on your shortlist that you'd like to see them and when. Some candidates may have already accepted another job. If so, then wish them luck.
- Be prepared to send directions to interviewees.
- Warn security or reception so that they can park and enter the building. Giving out a list of candidate names and likely arrival times means they can also be greeted by name.
- If someone is unusually rude over the phone or on the way into the building, then make a mental note of it. Do you want them to be representing your business or working within your team?
- Consider where they will wait if they're early. Interviewees are often very early.
- Will you be offering them tea or coffee? Who will fetch those drinks?
- Have you got some water on hand for the interview?
- Where can they use the facilities and are they clean?
- What chair are you planning to offer them to sit on? Is it clean?
- Hold all your calls and switch off your cell phone. If your email makes an annoying ping, turn it off. Try not to interview from behind a desk.
- If you are in a closed office make sure other workers don't pop in and interrupt you. Place a large note on your door – "Interviews in progress" – if necessary.
- Do you wish to conduct a skills test or work-based test of some kind? Who will do this? Warn the candidates about this.
- Think about your own appearance. On interviewing days you must look neat and tidy. You don't have to wear a suit if that's not your normal work attire, but you do have

to look professional. If you look like you don't care then guess what the interviewee will conclude?

That was seven steps before an interviewee even walks in but all these steps are crucial for zeroing in on that ideal future employee and minimizing risk.

CONDUCTING INTERVIEWS

> *Stitch up. It was a stitch up. They filmed hours of material and most of it is a good bloke doing a good job at work and the one time I accidentally head-butted an interviewee makes it to the program. You're gonna look like a prat. You head-butt a girl on telly and you're labeled a prat.*
> *Ricky Gervais as David Brent in* The Office, *BBC TV*

I've interviewed a lot of people and I know I've made some awful mistakes. I sometimes went into interviews without having read their paperwork. I know they could tell just as I could always tell when it happened to me. I sometimes cringe at the gaffes I've made. And having been interviewed for various jobs, full-time and short-term, and consulting contracts, I'm also very aware of the feelings of hope and disappointment involved, and of the lasting impressions of competence that stay with the interviewee. Thankfully I never actually head-butted anyone and nor did anyone ever head-butt me.

To prevent all risk of head-butting, a simple interview structure is helpful. Yes, it's another seven-step process.

1. Create a friendly, relaxed atmosphere.

Greet the candidate with a firm handshake but don't break their hand.

Walk them through to the interview location and let them get comfortable. Ask them if there's anything they need. Tell them about the basic structure you're going to follow and introduce anyone else they might meet during the interview. The interview itself needs to be relaxed and friendly so that the person is as comfortable as possible and able to speak freely. Feeling intimidated or antagonized does not bring out the best in anyone.

2. Get the interviewee to do most of the talking.

Try to get them talking. Ask them why the role appealed to them. Why have they chosen this career, job or industry? Not everyone is career-oriented. Sometimes people just want a job to pay the bills. That might be fine in some roles but not a good sign for others.

Not every vacancy is an exciting opportunity for progression. However, you still want to find the best candidate so listen carefully as people tell you about their background, any aspirations and, importantly, the decisions they've made in their working life. A forty year old who still makes decisions based on what his mates say might be of some concern.

Whether any comment or answer really matters depends on the qualities you need for the role. Look for patterns. One answer does not generally give us a clear picture.

Be careful that you don't do too much talking or start chatting. It's an easy trap to fall into, especially if someone is painfully quiet or if you've realized this is definitely not the right person and feel obliged to fill the time. A colleague of mine has a problem with the entertaining candidates and literally forgets to interview them.

3. Make sure you ask your most important questions.

Go into those well thought-out questions that were written after the specs were decided and ask everyone those questions.

Try not to ask closed questions about abilities and experiences. Closed questions invite yes or no answers. They're good for checking facts but they're not very useful for giving you a picture of the person you might want to employ.

For example, if you ask, "Are you a good engineer?", then what do you think a person is going to say?

People don't give you perfect answers and they don't always answer the question you asked. So ask again a little differently. If you're getting nowhere, move on. Perhaps they don't have an answer but don't want to say so. Let them know they can come back later. We can all think of great answers on the way home.

Asking people to tell you about their strengths and weaknesses usually yields useless information. I know they're commonly used and I once thought I had to use them as well, but I still think they're pointless.

Keep things relevant and professional. You are linking your questions and the candidate's answers to the actual job that needs doing. Remember that your aim is to help them feel free to speak clearly, openly and honestly. React politely to everything they say. They should never sense that they gave a wrong answer or earned your disapproval.

Please don't test people out with a trick question that makes no sense or has no relevance to the job. For example, a manager once told me that he liked to ask people what kind of animal they'd like to be. There is no useful answer they can possibly give and nothing to be gained from that kind of questioning. What is he going to do if they say aardvark? I've heard this practice defended by bosses saying "I just like to see how they'll react." Interviewees are not laboratory rats. What message are you sending about how they'll be treated when they come to work for you?

An interviewer once told me all about his marital problems. I'm sure most bosses understand that an interviewee does not want, or need to hear about your personal problems. And don't bad-mouth your own company, gossip about another employee, or discuss the details of any other candidates.

4. Ask if they have any questions.

Ask the interviewee if they have any questions about the job or the business.

The more senior or responsible the role, the less you want to hear "What are the holidays and minimum hours?" Instead you want thoughtful and researched questions. In professional roles you would hope to hear ideas about solving some of your issues. At school-leaver level, interviewees may be shy and awkward. Temps passing through may not know or care about your glorious corporate history. Adjust your expectations.

5. Tell the interviewee the next steps.

Tell the interviewee what is happening and when they can expect to hear. For example, "We still have three people to interview but we expect to come back to you all by the end of the week."

If you're definitely interested, ask for the names and contact details of their referees now if they have not already listed them on a CV.

6. Say goodbye and escort them out.

Close off the interview politely.

Be careful not to say "When can you start?" because that sounds awfully close to a job offer and a verbal contract.

But you can say "If you were successful, when could you start?"

Always thank people for their time and make sure they can find their way back to the exit. They don't know your office or workplace and shouldn't be left to wander about feeling lost.

7. Write your notes immediately and discuss the interview with your partner if you have one.

At the end of the interview, when the candidate is well out of sight, write your notes. This is done after they're gone because it's extremely off-putting if you write a lot of notes in front of the interviewee. It's also poor practice to hold up a clipboard as if you're writing a long parking ticket. And if you write on your lap, be warned that a lot of people can read upside down.

Plan this writing and discussion time into the day. Don't try to remember ten interviews at the end of a day and then start your writing. It doesn't work and it's not fair.

And be very careful about where those notes end up. I learned to shred them as soon as I didn't need them.

You can always hold a second interview to ask those good follow-up questions, but if you call all your interviewees back for a second interview then you haven't done the best job first time around. You should only ever call back people who are extremely likely to be selected. And second interviews should be enough. Third and fourth interviews start entering the realms of cruel and unusual punishment.

Use the second interview to make absolutely sure the candidates really understand the role and what will be required of them. They can't understand that unless you are clear about it yourself.

You should at least be frank about what results are expected even if you don't know the means of getting there.

So the interviewing is over and now the decision-making begins.

MAKING A DECISION

These are just a few things to consider before you make a decision.

Did the interviewee demonstrate anything that was clearly worrying or inconsistent with what you need?

Do you want good standards of hygiene but noticed that they were very dirty or unkempt. Are you looking for a driver or traveling sales rep and did they mention they got lost trying to find you? Are you employing someone to handle your PR but discover they just picked a stupid fight in the car park with someone? These concerns could be directly relevant to their future performance in a role and should be noted now.

Has there been a bit of CV padding or were there blatant lies?

CV padding is common but there is a line between trying to sound a bit more interesting to a future employer and making fraudulent claims. For example, a common bit of padding is to write that reading is an interest, when only two books a year are read beside a pool. People will invariably write "travel" when they do the same sort of package holiday every year. Most applicants are guilty of making their lives look a bit more urbane than they really are, but recruiters tend to let a lot of that storytelling go by. Unfortunately there are people who will present qualifications that are faked or belong to someone else. That can constitute a dangerous fraud when medical and other qualifications are invented. It's happy camping for many when recruiters do not check qualifications and work experiences. Behavioral questions help us manage those risks, but so does thorough reference checking.

Does their self-perception vary widely from reality?

An applicant may state that they thrive on responsibility but exhibit absolutely no sign of taking responsibility in their lives. I've seen applicants who describe themselves as risk takers and produce a CV that shows years in a secure dead-end job. Someone who has superior interpersonal skills would never state that they had superior interpersonal skills.

What about people who have been fired, retrenched or possess CVs with gaps?

People can leave jobs and risk unemployment out of great frustration and disappointment. It is entirely possible that someone has worked for a terrible boss who does not give them a good reference. Good people can be fired, laid off, or have a clash with someone who was almost impossible to deal with. Good people can be unfairly accused of something. It is all possible.

But is there a *pattern* of being let go? Is the interviewee usually moving on because of clashes with other people? People who have been made redundant a few times might ring warning bells, or then again, they might have a CV that is a sign of the times or their industries. Mothers can have CVs that show gaps because they were caring for young children and older parents and in-laws. Increasingly people take gaps for travel and voluntary work. That might be stated on the CV or not, but travel and voluntary experiences can display initiative and resourcefulness. Sometimes I've found people unwilling to put down self-employment, temp jobs, casual or voluntary work, when it actually does them credit and brings a skill that might be needed.

Are there other concerns about this interviewee?

Someone who is moderately ambitious tends to produce a CV that shows a gradual ascent in responsibility and influence. Sideways moves might be made to gain experience, but if you see sudden drops in responsibility or illogical moves, you might wonder why this is so and you need to ask.

What about people who have run their own businesses and gone bankrupt?

There are a lot of them about and they can be gems. Consider this – they took a risk and tried to run a business. It's possible they learned other lessons too. They may even be among the more self-motivated candidates.

Consider a person's honesty.

If someone is upfront about having been let go, or straight about former bankruptcy, then this probably bodes well. They may still be your best candidate. They may even have a criminal record and you might decide it's not relevant to the job on offer. However, if you discover that they've lied, and it's significant, you may want to move on to the next candidate. If you only discover a serious lie after the person starts, and you believe it's too important and relevant to their new responsibilities, you can (normally) call their omission a breach of trust and end the contract.

Are you planning to conduct medicals or tests that are relevant to your business?

It's wise to have a medical for your final applicants, or even the person you selected if you're down to a single obvious choice. It should be policy if you're a large employer to put everyone through a pre-employment medical test. These are done at your expense but you can nominate the doctor or doctors involved.

What you *cannot* do, is single out one person for a medical because you have some suspicions about their health and not send the others.

As for tests, consider work-based tests that are a close match to the critical tasks the candidate would perform each day. If you can't find one, create something. They are one of the more effective ways of ensuring you have made a good choice. A classic example of a work-based test is a typing test and this is a legitimate test if you're employing an administrative assistant for example.

Physical boot camps or outward bound days where interviewees are pressured to do unusually stressful tasks ought to be illegal in my view. The only exception to this would be if it was a relevant work-based test because you were required to lead outdoor activities.

With regard to psychometric tests, I will state up front that I'm qualified to use Myers-Briggs and a few others that are not quite as reputable. I've had some great experiences with teams and individuals using Myers-Briggs for its intended purpose: as a springboard to conversation. I have a lot of respect for the decades of research that went into its creation and yet I would never use this indicator for recruitment and have lost consulting work because of this stance.

When HR people qualify to use the more robust psychometric tests, they generally sign a page saying they will not commit the ethical breach of misusing the test. For Myers and Briggs, using their indicator to make decisions about people's livelihoods was a clear ethical breach. But this is not just about ethics, although that's a good enough reason to question the trend of testing for employment.

I'm very well aware that there are many employers forcing candidates through psychometrics without the freedom to opt out, or offering to provide feedback. I'm also aware that many recruiters are not qualified to administer the tests and cannot provide a good explanation as to why the company is using the test. Far be it for me to stand in front of a gravy train, but may I just ask these four questions to the bosses and HR people who use these tests as a compulsory gateway for all job applicants:

1. Are you absolutely sure there is a proven, valid link between the results of the test you're giving and competence for a job?
2. Are you aware of the inherent biases and histories of discrimination these tests carry that punish certain groups, including the anxious? If so, is this sitting comfortably with claims you're making to value diversity and be an employer who will not tolerate discrimination?
3. Is it sitting comfortably with your personal notions of decency, fairness and rights to privacy if people have no option but to sit these tests if they want a job in your company and are then denied the right to any feedback from a competent assessor?
4. Is the person telling you the tests are able to predict a good fit for employment the same person who will profit from your use of the test?

Psychometric indicators can't tell you how a person will operate in a role within your business, or whether they will succeed or fail, become a rainmaker or rob the petty cash. What could possibly do this? The only good predictor of future behavior is past behavior and even that's not a rock solid guarantee.

There is a tenuous link between test results and any competency being assessed and I for one am not prepared to rely on it. In my opinion, you're far better off doing good interviews and reference checks. You also have the probation time in most contracts if you've made a mistake.

Perhaps Peter Drucker made the case more forcefully when he wrote "an employer has no business with a man's personality. Employment is a specific contract calling for a specific performance and nothing else. Any attempt to go beyond this usurpation – it's an immoral as well as illegal intrusion of privacy."

IQ or Intelligence Quotient testing is another quagmire for managers. I'll skip the ongoing arguments over the definitions of intelligence, whether the tests are fair or even likely to come up with an accurate result, and just warn you that that there is no great proven link between intelligence and likely success in a job, but there are plenty of concerns about the fairness and value in IQ tests.

Recruiters are only human.

If you feel stuck about making a final choice, then go back to your Job Spec and Person Spec. What did you decide were the critical qualities needed for this job? Now focus on what will matter versus what can be lived with. If someone is strong in a key requirement then this should tip the scales in their favor. If a weakness is not critical, it might be overlooked or helped with some training or coaching.

Beware of the Halo effect, which occurs when we take a shine to someone because they remind us of someone fabulous – ourselves! It's also called "recruiting in our own image."

We push their papers forward and say "He'd be great" or "She and I just clicked so she'll be perfect." Highly qualified, well-dressed and well-spoken candidates may be very skilled at interviews and disastrous for your business. You have to train yourself to look beyond the veneer.

The opposite of the Halo effect is when we think we're very unlike the person we're interviewing and start rejecting them because of their differences.

We wrinkle our face and say "I'm not sure why but I can't see her fitting in here."

Or "There's just something about him I can't seem to warm to."

Are you selecting someone because you found them attractive? It does happen and can confuse you. Are you rejecting them because they were unattractive?

OK, you didn't particularly like them in the first minute. Are you being fair? Are you sure that there isn't a personal prejudice seeping through?

Gut reactions are fine but back up your intuition with good questions during the interview or perhaps in a second interview. Keep those specifications close by and be mindful of these very human traps. Remember – your challenge is to make the very best match of your key selection criteria against candidates.

Making the right decisions adds value to the business. Making careless decisions can cost you dearly. Smaller businesses are more closely attuned to this notion. If you are recruiting in a larger business, try pretending that it's your money that is at stake.

Don't delegate the decision. Make your own choice.

You might be the boss, but if there's another manager who'll work with this person then get their views. Ideally, they were part of the interviewing process with you.

Ask for views but don't delegate the choice to any outside consultant or agency unless their profits are tied to yours.

Their interest is not in the survival and success of your business. Will they feel any pain at all if they are wrong? An external consultant can never compete with a level-headed boss who clearly understands what he or she wants and is prepared to go through the process carefully.

*

OK – so you've made a choice. That's not the end of it.

Manage the rejections.

Making the call to the successful candidate can be great fun, especially when people are relieved or excited and you can hear their joy over the line. I love that job!

If people attended interviews with you then they should also be phoned with the news that they were unsuccessful. These calls are no fun at all but it is the decent thing to do. It's cowardly to drop them a letter. They invested a lot in your search and a call is more personal. If they were very close then tell them so. Is there a chance to keep them interested in case something else comes up? If you would want the person to apply again in future, tell them so.

Let everyone else go if you are still holding other applications.

It is really hard getting rejection letters. It's even worse when you don't hear at all and too many e-recruitment systems are a dispiriting black hole for job applicants. Never leave people wondering and saying "they never even wrote back." Thank people for their time and interest. Wish them luck.

You might be asked "Where did I go wrong?" or "Can you give me some specific feedback?" I wouldn't touch those questions with a barge pole. You're not obliged to say anything at all.

You can always say something constructive about a positive attribute they possess, but stay polite and tread very carefully. "We had a lot of good candidates and you were unsuccessful on this occasion." Remember that you don't have to defend your decision to a failed applicant – or their mother.

Sometimes I have felt desperate to tell someone about how they really let themselves down at the interview, but I still won't do it. It's just too easy to be misconstrued and you may find yourself facing accusations of being unfair or even discriminating. Remember, this is still a PR exercise and this person remains a spokesperson for the way your business deals with people.

Never make a statement around personality or character: "We thought the other guy had a more outgoing personality." "We felt you would struggle with handling pressure." How do you know? How can you prove that? You're on very thin ice making such statements and yet innocent recruiters will make these kinds of comments.

If the person already works for you then you don't want to destroy their motivation and interest in the business. It may be they will be ready for the promotion next time. Is there something they can do to improve their chances? Above all, manage this disappointment carefully because the unsuccessful employee may well have to work with your new candidate and that can be tricky.

ONBOARDING OR INDUCTING NEW STARTERS

Always let the successful candidate know first. If they've changed their mind then you might have your second or third choice person to go to. Be prepared for a change of heart. It's possible that some other employer has beaten you to them. They were in the job market after all. It can also be that the person went through this exercise in order to get a pay rise from their existing employer. It happens.

Every employee should have a contract of employment and ideally this should be signed before they start work. If the new employee does not have a contract before they arrive then it should be given to them very promptly after they start.

Inducting or onboarding are just terms for an organized welcome that covers the basic knowledge they will need including things like workplace health and safety. This doesn't need to be a series of formal speeches that goes on for hours. It can be a one to one "walk and talk" exercise. Every employee who comes to work for you should be properly introduced into the business, whether it employs two people or 2,000.

Inducting is more important than most of us realize, because human beings remember starts and finishes.

Some basics for managing this properly:

- Make sure the new starter knows the date and time they are expected to start.
- Inform security that they are coming so they can be let through the gate or building.
- Decide who is going to meet and greet them and see them to their work area.

- Organize their work area prior to the arrival.
- Make sure they are clear about who they can go to for help in these early days, if their supervisor is not about.
- Let everyone who will see this person, know that they are arriving so that they can be greeted by name. It's really basic.
- Make sure they know the location of the toilets, what happens at breaks and lunchtime and where to get a drink of water, tea or coffee. Where can they store food?

There is often a legal requirement to make sure a new employee understands about fire drills, hazards, first aid and any health and safety or security information. Even if the law doesn't force you into this, do it anyway.

Never put new people into new jobs unless there is a great deal of support. Newcomers must go into established places or work processes, where results and controls are known and help is immediately available to them.

Make sure a new starter has work to get on with when they arrive. To go through all the work to find the right person and then leave them scratching their heads when they begin is a rapid drain on their goodwill and motivation on day one. Think through the plan of work for your new employee carefully. It's normal and desirable that they're keen to get their teeth into a challenge but don't swamp them either.

Check on how they are getting on.

In the early days, a casual inquiry will suffice. After a few weeks you may want to have a follow-up discussion with the new employee and with their immediate boss if that isn't you.

- Are they doing well? If so, then tell them so.
- Are they struggling? If so, what are they struggling with?
- What help is needed?
- Has there clearly been a mistake in hiring this person? It's not typical, but sometimes you might let someone go in the first month or before the probation period is up. Give them a real chance but if it's clearly not going to work out, it's better for both parties if the contract is ended quickly. Go back to your processes just the same. Did you get something very wrong in your recruiting?

Some final notes on this very important process ...

Generally the people you interview are understandably trying to put on a good face and a certain amount of acting is going on. The majority of people will be very pleasant and their honesty will impress you. You can also learn a lot. I have met some fascinating people through interviewing.

You'll meet people who are very modest and might be terrific at what they do but clearly hate the whole selling atmosphere of interviews. There are people who do not express themselves very well. Be prepared to be patient and you might uncover some treasures.

Be wary of people who behave with a sense of entitlement, who are somewhat aggressive and clearly believe you're lucky to have them in front of you. This is a very clear signal about the way they will interact with people – and perhaps your customers – on a daily basis.

And please, do not conduct panel interviews with three or more people. Aside from the waste of resources, the interviewee is made to feel they are defending themselves against a criminal charge. Good management is about making decisions and taking responsibility. Increasing the number of interviewers does not make discrimination less likely. It makes groupthink more likely.

Recruitment is a critical business process. It deserves to be treated as such.

Why do so many businesses fill their ranks with Yes Men? How do business units or teams make decisions or follow orders that cause them to go over cliffs lemming-style? How is it that businesses can feel so friendly and comfortable and yet be underperforming or failing?

A good boss hires for strength and to ensure the survival of the business. They look for skills and personal qualities that are missing from the team or from themselves. An insecure boss hires the candidate who doesn't shine too much. Don't hire people because they make you feel less threatened.

It also saddens me to hear managers say that they take whoever is sent to them from agencies or human resources, and believe that that's the way things are and it cannot get better. "Sometimes you just need someone with a pulse and you don't care" they'll say, and then complain loudly about high turnover, low morale and poorly skilled, even dangerously inept employees. If you find that people are resigning quite early on in their employment, then find out why.

Let go of the mythical notion that you ought to be able to sum up people in an instant. There is no substitute for the planning and thought put into interviews and no excuse for abdicating this to other people who will not feel the consequences of a mistake.

Go back to the first question every time – what does your business need? Your business will be run by people and invariably, salaries will be your greatest cost. Take great care and thought over the people coming into it, whether you run a research lab or a hamburger stall. Every single vacancy is an opportunity to improve the quality of your business. Every careless choice will result in loss, cost, and wasted opportunity.

CHAPTER SIX

KEEPING PEOPLE

HOW DO YOU KEEP GOOD PEOPLE?
THE PRACTICAL REALITIES WITHIN THEORIES
WHERE DOES RECOGNITION FIT IN TO MOTIVATION?
WHERE DOES MONEY FIT IN TO MOTIVATION?
WHERE DOES SECURITY FIT IN TO MOTIVATION?
WHERE DOES FEAR FIT IN TO MOTIVATION?
INDOCTRINATION AND DIGNITY

*

HOW DO YOU KEEP GOOD PEOPLE?

The short answer is – you don't. This chapter is not about guaranteeing that good employees never leave. People move on. It happens. You can't grab them around the ankles and start crying when they resign. Well, you can, but it looks a bit desperate.

This is about keeping good people performing while they're with you and reducing what is sometimes called regrettable turnover – when you lose the people who really help your business to succeed. Or when you lose the people you want to grab around the ankles.

I've heard a lot of managers say they'd like to know how to motivate people. Clearly many of us think this is possible so it's worth pointing out the major limitations.

- We don't really motivate other people. People motivate themselves.
- People are motivated to satisfy their own needs, not ours.
- Everyone has needs, even if their greatest need is to be left alone.
- People may not always express their needs very clearly.
- Our needs change. Sometimes they change very quickly.
- Once a need is reasonably well satisfied it's often replaced with another need. The individual decides what is reasonable.
- The term "never satisfied" fits just about everyone.
- Some people will never feel they have enough of a particular need, such as status, a sense of belonging, or money.
- People can work in what appears to be a great workplace with many of their needs provided for and yet consistently under-perform.
- People can work in appalling circumstances, starving in a garret or working for free, and be highly motivated and effective in what they do.
- No one has all the answers to this subject.
- There's lots of money to be made pretending that you have the answers.

We are motivated to satisfy our own needs, and this is why

one person cannot directly motivate another. Motivation is an internal drive, not an externally applied push. Only the individual can decide whether a need has been met, or whether a reward or punishment is worth changing behavior for. Only the individual can decide to increase their effort.

It's an old saying, but a useful one to remember – you can lead a horse to water but you can't make it drink.

We have been given some useful ideas about human needs from theorists such as Maslow, MacGregor and Herzberg. It's just that what they, and all the other motivation theorists cannot do, what most never promised to do, is give you the answers for quickly and successfully motivating your particular employees right now. So, when you see a book or a talk titled *How to Motivate People* or *The Secrets of Motivation* or anything that promise s to give you the inside scoop on getting more out of other people, then you are dealing with snake oil.

But gosh it's tempting, isn't it? It's as optimistic as the products that claim to take ten years off your face. And just like those products, there will always be eager buyers in the motivation game. When absolute answers aren't available, a bit of juju will do.

This could, therefore, be a very short chapter and end here, but that's not very useful.

A more realistic goal is to find ways to create a work environment where employees believe they are satisfying their needs while accomplishing the results that they were asked to achieve.

There are no answers. Just, at best, a few
guesses that might be worth a try.

Tom Peters, author of In Search of
Excellence

Some managers become too concerned with motivating poor or mediocre performers, whereas it's the good performers that deserve the greater focus. Too often, bosses ignore their best employees in the belief that these people are "covered" or that their loyalty and commitment can be taken for granted. "I don't need to do anything with that guy", a manager may insist, "he's not my worry." But the fastest way to create a demotivating environment is to ignore the people who do good work, and make a great deal of fuss over the people who don't.

Two other sure-fire ways to create a lousy work environment are to let people work in the dark – never tell them how they're doing or what's going on, and nitpick – just tell people when they've done something wrong but stay silent when they've done good work.

Employers can certainly provide carrots and sticks but there are no guarantees. What one person sees as an opportunity, another person might perceive as a burden. I've seen employees almost curl up on the floor in terror because they'd been invited to attend a training course, while other employees were quite desperate to be sent to the same thing. When a boss announces a social event for everyone to attend there will be employees whose hearts sink at the thought of having to put on a party face and genuinely feel that this is a punishment.

However the situation is not at all hopeless. There's a great deal you can do in spite of all the limitations. It all begins – and doesn't everything – with talking and listening.

Needs are a moving target. Think about your need for food. Think about your need for human company. This means that we have to ask people what they want from their work from time to time. Not on a daily basis, of course – that would be a bit weird. And we can't ask them once in their working lives, because they might change their priorities. So we have to try to link up their reasonable wants and needs with our pressing need for a result. The largest piece in the puzzle is being comfortable in asking people what they want. A frequent mistake is made when managers assume they know without asking. They might assume all people are chasing the same things, or they assume people want the same things that interest them.

We have to learn to ask the questions such as:

- What do you find interesting in this work?
- What are you looking for from this job?
- What do need from me as a manager?
- Where do you see yourself in the next few years?
- What do you need to succeed in this role?

People aren't stupid. They don't expect a large bonus or parcel of company shares if they're flipping burgers. People usually ask for very basic things, for example, a market-level livable wage. They will often hope for, but not necessarily ask for, intangible things such as:

- Flexibility, especially if the employee is caring for others
- Fairness
- A fair chance at available promotions
- Interesting work
- Some variety in the work
- Tactful and discreet feedback
- News about how the business is doing

- Help and support when it's needed
- Timely news about what's going on
- Opportunities to develop skills and get some training
- Genuine and relevant appreciation for good work done.

Another common mistake is assuming that it's only going to be a conversation about money. There are so many things that can be offered besides money. You'd be surprised at what is appealing about your workplace. For example, there are some very well-known brand name organizations that need large numbers of salespeople but have few opportunities for promotion, and they don't pay very well. Nevertheless, they attract eager recruits because they provide excellent training. Recruits know that when they leave these organizations they'll be attractive to other sales companies who are not able or willing to train and develop staff from scratch.

Very simple things can be prove to be a drawcard. Some companies have found that a "pets at work" policy is a surprisingly low-cost motivator. Allowing the staff to get away a bit early on a Friday might be something you can offer. Some managers let employees take extra leave without pay, which can be a mutual gain if the business has peaks and troughs.

One objection to having a conversation about motivation is a fear that asking may open a door to being manipulated or put under an obligation. I recall one manager saying, "What if they ask for promotion? It's dead men's shoes around here and I'd be lying to them if I said otherwise. If I'm honest, then they'll leave. I'd rather not ask."

If you promise promotion and the employee realizes – as he or she inevitably will – that this is not going to happen, then you're going to be seen as dishonest. Being a straight talker is appreciated and it builds trust. People are free to leave. Better they leave thinking highly of you and the time they spent in your workplace.

Is there room for some lateral thinking? If an employee seeks promotion then maybe there's a chance to help them get ready for the next step. Tell your employee that you would recommend them if you could. Everyone likes recognition and appreciation. If you work for a larger business and you can't offer promotion in your team then ask around on their behalf.

But don't assume they will ask for the impossible. Don't avoid having the conversation.

THE PRACTICAL REALITIES WITHIN THEORIES

Most of the theories about creating a motivating workplace tend to fall within one of three groups.

First, there is the idea that in order to get greater productivity or quality out of employees, you need to provide better working conditions. Moving to a brand new office with a better canteen would be an example. These are the paternalistic theories. The word paternalistic tells us that this is about taking care of everyone.

Scientific management theories are about tying a reward to the actual result achieved. This suggests that people are inclined to work harder if they are personally gaining a reward through their efforts. Commissions and bonuses tied to results are an example.

A third school of thought maintains that employees are already motivated and a boss only needs to let people get on with the work and get out of their way. Employees are inspired by participation and want to be free to make decisions about how they do the actual work. These are called participative theories.

All three ideas have potential and all have limitations. Most bosses will try to create a workplace that combines rewards and incentives from all three beliefs. Completely neglecting any of the ideas could spell trouble but expecting great surges in productivity from any particular effort is usually naive.

Are paternalistic ideas useful?

With these rewards, every player gets a prize. That is their beauty and their downfall. Typical across the board, paternalistic benefits might include free parking, a nice office, a good Christmas party, uniforms, clean facilities, free coffee and tea, arranged discounts, a good pension scheme, health care benefits, and facilities such as gyms and childcare.

There's a huge and creative range of paternalistic rewards that companies can provide. Employers may not even realize that these kinds of rewards are appreciated. For example, I worked in a company where it was common to find young staff occupying the office on the weekend. Some of them were simply having a sleep in peace, while some were using the meeting rooms to study in peace or type up assignments. In another company employees were able to purchase used fleet cars. Employees can appreciate the freedom to dress casually. I have frequently heard employees express their loyalty and gratitude to an employer for showing understanding and flexibility during an illness or family problem. But here's the thing – gratitude, enjoyment and loyalty are not necessarily going to result in someone doing better or doing more. Existing theories have given us many ideas that may be worth trying but as yet, no one has produced the strong proof that there is some consistent predictor of performance when it comes to human beings.

The problem is that paternalistic rewards are equally enjoyed. An employee attains these perks whether they are a complete slacker or bringing in fabulous results. It's not easy for a rational individual to see why they should raise their personal performance levels just because new office chairs have arrived.

So why bother? Why not turn off the heating and leave the paintwork to chip and fade for the next few decades? If we provide these things and they have no particular effect on the result, why not provide the minimum and run a sweatshop? Why not cancel the annual party?

The reason to have some of these things in place – if they are not legally required – is because they have an impact on attracting the quality of staff that you want. They may influence people's decisions to leave and help you keep good employees. Of course, a great workplace may also make life so good that your poor performers will never want to leave either, unless you make other arrangements.

Universal benefits can help keep morale at room temperature, but that really is better than going below zero. An affordable and clean place to have lunch may not make anyone go crazy to get their work results through the roof, but it might stop people getting cheesed off. It might save you other costs as well. To use the same example, keeping people at work to have their lunch has benefits. It reduces the safety risks that arise from leaving work during the day and encourages people to socialize. It gives you a place to hold meetings and social events. Good managers will still offer paternalistic motivators without expecting miracles in results.

Providing something for everyone comes with a warning label – it could create a problem should you ever have to take it away. In workplaces where previous managers have been overly generous in good times, it's hard for anyone else trying to rein in costs. I've heard griping that has gone on for years over the cancellation of extra leave, expensive social outings, perks for families, heavily subsidized food, and so on. Think ahead when you give a reward to everyone. You may need to stress that it's a one-off gesture. If you must take something away, explain why. And if you're making cuts, make sure the pain is shared. Certainly no one wants to lose something they really are entitled to, such as their own pension.

Are scientific rewards worth considering?

Rewards given to individuals according to their results fall under the scientific management banner, and all the critical lessons about reinforcement of behavior are repeated here – human beings can alter their behavior based on what is rewarded or ignored.

Scientific management is all about reinforcement of the desired behavior of the individual. A simple example is this: I'm employed to pick apples, and at day's end I'm paid only for the number of filled bags of apples. My reward is directly tied to my performance.

If I picked ten bags of apples, and the person next to me managed one bag but was paid the same, would I feel motivated to work as hard the next day? People have a curious habit of adjusting their performance level downward when the rewards are strictly consistent, and so rewarding individuals for their outcomes is the surest way to improve productivity. This is the basic and fairly rational argument behind scientific management theories, and our own eyes and years at work can tell us that this school of thinking is on to something.

In work that is more complicated than apple picking, you can see the same cynical feeling that affects the energetic apple-picker pervading the work atmosphere. We might continue to work hard if we think that, for example, job security or some other gain is more likely for us, but if benefits are applied equally to everyone and promotion and pay are linked to time served, then it's hard to imagine why anyone would strain themselves.

This adjusting-down behavior is the reason why many large bureaucratic employers, with promotion based on years of service, often struggle to get highly effective motivated workforces. When a business does not differentiate between people's contributions at all, there is a kind of dull lethargy that you can often feel in the air as you walk about. Staff can exude a "can't win-don't care" attitude. Certainly, if people are rewarded and promoted regardless of performance, then we can't expect a business will do anything other than stagnate. One of the few enduring great thinkers on management, Peter Drucker, expresses it perfectly:

> As we have known for a long time, people in organizations tend to behave as they see others being rewarded. And when the rewards go to nonperformance, flattery, or to mere cleverness, the organization will soon decline into nonperformance, flattery or cleverness.

Most managers who want their business to do well will try to find a way to reward individuals for their effort. And tying rewards to performance is very common. Examples include:

- Promotions based on merit
- Promotions based on results
- Bonuses or commissions tied to results
- Extra time off for good work
- Perks that are tied to grades if promotion is based on merit
- Prizes and awards handed out for good work or achievement
- Training and development opportunities offered to achievers or high potentials
- Trips as prizes
- Preference on the roster for good results

Just like the paternalistic rewards, little things can mean a lot – a bunch of flowers, a bottle of wine or a box of chocolates in recognition of effort. You rarely have to go through policy committees to grant small rewards, like telling someone to take an extra-long lunch break or knock off an hour early for a great effort, and most people appreciate these gestures. I say "most people" because there are always whiners who will even complain about freebies and perks. You shouldn't let that noise bother you terribly. You certainly shouldn't let them distract you from recognizing good performers.

Scientific management reminds us that people are a bit self-centered and generally want to know what's in it for them. If a person believes they'll be rewarded for achievement then it's more likely they'll be interested in achieving. It has a clean logic to it and is often a very successful means of keeping good people interested.

However, it's not perfect. An extract from the wonderful poem, *The Battery Hen* by Pam Ayres, may give you a hint about the potential flaws.

> I see the time and motion clock
> Is sayin' nearly noon
> I spec' me squirt of water
> Will come flyin' at me soon
> And then me spray of pellets
> Will nearly break me leg
> And I'll bite the wire nettin'
> And lay one more bloody egg

Of course, employees are not battery hens but if you're only rewarding for results, and ignoring the work environment and the needs for freedom and participation, then you run the terrible risk of treating people like egg producers and setting up some very unappealing problems.

Time and motion consultants were proponents of scientific management and they are often blamed for the demise of craftsmanship. Scientific management was the source of mass-production techniques. Today, strictly piece-rate work can often be found in sectors of industry that go way below the legal minimums on wages and conditions for employees.

Rewarding individuals is vitally important, but setting up performance systems that are fair and intelligent is no simple thing. There are genuine pitfalls to dangling the dollar in front of employees, even where the work conditions are good.

- Rewarding the individual *only* can unwittingly fuel the breakdown of teamwork. People may not help each other, share information, or do anything that distracts them from their own targets.

- Quality can suffer. If we are paid for each bag of apples we pack, we might not take the time to check the amount of debris or rotten produce being thrown in. If I am paid only to finalize mortgages, I may not care to check whether the person applying can pay it off.
- Standards can drop. We may not particularly care about the reputation of the company as we chase performance targets, so it can trigger unethical behavior from some employees.
- We might be less interested in honest service and assisting customers if the reward comes only for ringing up the sale.
- We may come to work when we shouldn't. If our illness is contagious, then it may spread to other employees, their families and to customers. We may also be a safety risk.
- We may continue to work when we're injured, aggravate a problem and be a risk to ourselves and others.
- We may cut corners, take shortcuts with our work or work unsafely because we are chasing a reward and how we get there was not deemed important.

What happens if you only reward hard work and long hours?

In most workplaces, you can find employees who are terribly busy and seemingly rushed off their feet, but are not terribly effective. Similarly, you can find people who seem a bit laidback but are completely focused and get things done.

If you pay for hours worked without considering how long the work should take, there may be trouble ahead. When people are paid for their time and not questioned or managed about the effective use of it, it's in their interests to stretch out the task. If overtime is available without too much scrutiny, people will claim they need to work overtime. Cancel overtime, and more effective work practices will develop very rapidly.

If you keep promoting people who put in long hours but fail to look at the results they achieve, you may develop a culture where everyone feels they have to work late to get anywhere. Good time management principles will go out the window and you can forget about asking people to identify wasted effort. Employees who exert more effort to get to the required result are no different to cars that burn too much fuel to go the same distance. They are costing you time and resources. Employees wanting to improve their work-life balance are an increasingly bigger group, and enabling them to achieve this balance could be one of the smarter incentives on offer for good performers.

Rewarding the team effort

If we only reward individuals then teamwork can suffer. Some bosses find ways to tie the results of the whole team to the individual's reward and add them together. Indeed, some businesses operate schemes that reward the employee for how well the entire business is doing. This connection between pay packet and business success can also produce a greater interest in cost savings and opportunities as employees now see a link between how the business does and how they benefit directly.

Performance Management Systems

Performance management schemes are absolutely loaded with potential pitfalls. That doesn't mean they should be completely avoided (and they have other uses besides administering rewards) but careful thought is required.

Opinion is divided on the overall worth (in large companies) of submitting everyone to a process of a performance conversation once or twice a year. On the one hand, the conversation about performance ought to be ongoing rather than being viewed, as they frequently are, as a compliance exercise driven by the HR department. An employee should always be clear about what they need to do, the standard required from them and the positive consequences for success. On the other hand, many employees complain that they never have such conversations, that the boss talks "at them" and not "with them" about setting goals, the long term, and performance, and so a more formal process (that the boss must complete) is appreciated.

Performance management processes in larger employers are generally tied to rewards and any decent reward system must be one that employees can understand clearly and agree with. As soon as bosses seem to make reward deliberations in secret, or make promotion decisions that can't be fathomed or questioned, the potentially stimulating aspect of the scheme is gone. It has to be fair and transparent.

Targets have to be rational. SMART goals are Specific, Measurable, Agreed, Realistic and Time-based goals. Any employee needs to understand how they will be measured. If you like to set tougher goals or "stretch targets", as they are sometimes called, make sure they don't become demoralizing ones instead.

Targets set and the final results achieved must not be secret information. Imagine running toward a high jump bar and having no idea how high it was set?

Further, you cannot penalize people for things outside their control. Consider the dangers of rewarding doctors for every prescription they wrote. What if a doctor was financially penalized for every patient who died? How would that be fair, given that patients frequently ignore the advice of medical professionals? If teachers are rewarded for A students, how many report cards will begin to look too wonderful? How easy will it be for a child with special needs to get into a school?

Consider what you might accidentally reward. What might people do to reach their targets? Might they behave dangerously to meet a time target? Might they fudge the results or hide problems?

Managing in the future will be less about watching people and more about assessing their results. Trusting people will be critical, so better recruitment becomes critical. Good communication skills will be even more important in order to delegate effectively. And setting up transparent, intelligent and fair reward systems will be essential.

This sub-topic of rewards and performance could take up an entire book. Rewards help to shape a culture because they can shape behavior. Rewards are reinforcement. When there are problem behaviors or just odd quirks in a work culture, we can look at how these problems or quirks became entrenched by looking at the people who typically advance through the system. Every time an employee is promoted the business is sending a signal about behavior that's truly valued, and – as we are creatures who move in the direction of satisfying our needs – those behaviors will be copied.

You are entitled to distinguish between people's efforts when you manage a business. You are, after all, trying to make your business as successful as it can be. Don't let anyone tell you that rewarding individuals is discrimination, unless your rewards are based on favoritism and exclude certain groups from ever being able to compete fairly. In fact, a robust and well-managed system of rewards for performance will chip away at discrimination and promote merit.

Build in motivators and incentives that encourage and reward good performers and the behaviors you value. If the whiners become unhappy then that's great. It might push them to look elsewhere. Clearly send the message that rewards follow valued results and professional behaviors, and you begin to create a performance culture and change the workplace for the better.

Participation

Participative theories suggest that real participation is a reward in itself. Under this banner is the idea people like to see results and don't need to be actively motivated to do well.

> I've always had an easy time directing actors because I always hire ones that are great and mostly what I do is stay out of their way.
>
> Woody Allen

A boss can provide what is needed to do the task and get out of the way. This also suggests that people want to be free to think, be able to make decisions and have influence and full involvement in what they do. Employees may want to determine their own way of getting to the result. This is where the shift to empowering people came from. In theory, enthusiasm and higher productivity will follow. The idea that people have an intrinsic need to work and take pride in that work may sound a bit old-fashioned, but if you doubt it, spend some time with the long-term unemployed.

If you head down this road to try to motivate others you'll be giving employees as much control over their work as possible. It will be as if you're creating a small army of self-employed people on the payroll.

Some bosses would hear this and insist that people must be watched over, that they won't work unless they have to. But consider how many people need to be prodded every few minutes to do anything – they are few and far between and you need to deal with those rare cases as a disciplinary issue. Very few people buzz around all day, but the truly useless loafer is not common. And if you have a lot of them in your workplace, then why is that so?

The vast majority of employees like to feel useful and will often take pride in what they do, want their workplace to succeed, and work to see things change for the better. Barbara Ehrenreich noted this in her book, *Nickel and Dimed*, working among the lowest paid employees in the US economy.

> While I encountered some cynics and plenty of people who had learned to budget their energy, I never met an actual slacker or, for that matter, a drug addict or thief. On the contrary, I was amazed and sometimes saddened by the pride people took in jobs that rewarded them so meagerly, either in wages or recognition. Often, in fact, these people experienced management as an obstacle to getting the job done. Waitresses chafed at managers' stinginess toward the customers; housecleaners resented the time constraints that sometimes made them cut corners; retail workers wanted the floor to be beautiful, not cluttered with excess stock as management required. Left to themselves, they devised systems of cooperation

and work sharing; when there was a crisis, they rose to it. In fact it was often hard to see what the function of management was, other than to exact obeisance.

Participation does require a shift in attitude and behavior, but it does not require a massive investment. It can be made up of benefits such as:

- Flexibility
- Choices wherever possible
- Being asked for an opinion
- Responsibility
- The chance to set personal goals
- Clear expectations
- Freedom to design tasks
- The removal of barriers to achieving targets
- Involvement in successful or high-status work
- Having improvements accepted and implemented – even small ones
- Being given new and challenging tasks and activities
- Being given the authority to achieve the result

From a business point of view it's easy to see why participation is an attractive concept. It's a great benefit to have employees who bring ideas, methods and suggestions, or who question processes and want to make improvements for the benefit of the business. It frees up managers' time and usually means you can reduce the size of management.

Think of the alternative: a workplace where no one asks "Why?"

Why do you file these forms?

We've always filed them.
But who needs these forms? What is their purpose?
I just file them.
Yes, but who asks for them? What would happen if you
didn't file them?
But they're needed for the archives.

Or this conversation:
Why do you have this meeting?
It's the Monday meeting.
Yes, but what does it do? What does it achieve?
It's the Monday meeting. We've always had it.
What would happen if you cancelled it?
Are you saying it should move to a Tuesday?

These exchanges were real. I don't believe the employee with
the files and the manager with the entrenched meeting were
stupid people but it was clear they had not been reinforced to
ask why. It's frustrating to work where people defend the need
to do meaningless work.

> *Most men would feel insulted if it were*
> *proposed to employ them in throwing*
> *stones over a wall, and then throwing them*
> *back merely that they might earn their*
> *wages. But many are no more worthily*
> *employed now.*
>
> *Henry David Thoreau*

Participation is about encouraging people to think beyond
their job description and question accepted patterns of
doing things. This causes some anxiety for those who cling to

habits and rules, but since such folk are often in need of a shake-up, it's no bad thing. If it turns out that someone's role doesn't match their job description, or that their pay does not reflect their contribution, then make the necessary changes and keep the motivation going. It's the result that matters most.

With a bit of encouragement, employees can be surprisingly free with ideas for improving methods, systems, and all aspects of a business that bosses had assumed were theirs to worry about alone.

Everyone's smart at something. Tremendous ideas come from unlikely places. The person doing the task may have a great suggestion for improving it. Field Marshal Montgomery thought it was wise to watch the laziest, smartest soldiers for clues about valid shortcuts.

We know that inventiveness has nothing to do with class, gender, age, race, qualifications or school grades. Indeed people with a knack for innovative thinking are bound to be outside the norm. Albert Einstein did not speak until he was four years old and couldn't read until he was seven. One of his teachers described him as "mentally slow, unsociable and adrift forever in his foolish dreams." He failed the entrance exam for the Federal Institute of Technology in Zurich on his first attempt.

The person who asks why and comes up with ideas may not even be directly involved in the task. Eli Whitney began to think about the cotton gin while he was tutoring a plantation owner's children. Watching the labor-intensive work going on outside the classroom window, he imagined there had to be a better way.

*

Does participation work? Just like paternalistic rewards and scientific management, there is a benefit and there are limitations.

Participation does sit well in creative, professional workplaces, where the work methods and processes are constantly improving. It suits people who are fairly mature and had a school report that probably said "works well without supervision." Where people are committed to their own goals and bristle at being micro-managed, participation seems to be a good solution.

But not every kind of job is open to innovation and freedom. Delivering the post may allow someone to decide the time of day they deliver and the route they'll take, but the physical task of shoving the papers through letterboxes is fairly well established and it's hard to think of any more creativity that could be applied to the job, aside from new ideas for making the journey more interesting or dealing with aggressive dogs. There are assembly-line jobs and businesses with very tightly written processes that don't give individuals a lot of scope for freedom, other than the chance to change roles about.

However, participation theories still suggest that all staff on the assembly line will have a desire to know more about what's going on, and have more of a say in the overall workplace wherever possible. For example, there may be room to contribute to a safety or social committee, or to solving the problems of variation.

It's important to think about the individuals who won't welcome the chance to make a lot of decisions about their work. You can unwittingly place pressure on some employees who struggle to come up with ideas. I've encountered people working in pretty monotonous jobs who loved what they were doing because it was an escape from having too much responsibility. A garbage collector I met had once run a wholesale food business employing about twenty people. "I love this job," he said. "I come to the depot and no one cares who you are or where you come from. I know exactly what I have to do. I go out on the trucks, get some exercise and go home. My afternoons are free. I wear what I like. I do not have to think about the work once I've left it." Having come close to a breakdown trying to save his business from bankruptcy, you could understand why he was attracted to this workplace. When the shift was over, that was it.

The level playing field that participation breeds is an attraction for some and a reason to be afraid for others. Some bosses are too quick to insist that their employees don't want to think and have a say, when in fact, staff are frustrated and want to offer sensible improvements.

Participation encourages managers to get out of the way, or at least avoid hovering over people and keeping too much to themselves. Managers who are unwilling to credit other people with intelligence and insight will struggle to adopt participation motivators in their workplace. Trust is a big issue. Another inhibitor of participation could be the managers who need therapy before they can start accepting constructive ideas and suggestions from people they always felt were there to do as they were told.

Managing in the future will be less about watching people and more about assessing their results. Just ensure that you don't completely abdicate the role of management. You still need to plan, lead, organize and control, but with participation you might be able to involve more people in those activities. Certainly they can be as aware of the plans, organizing systems and controls as you are. Participation gives you real time to lead and the ability to let go of the task. That is an incentive for many bosses to give it a try.

WHERE DOES RECOGNITION FIT IN TO MOTIVATION?

I was setting up a training room one morning and didn't realize that one of the factory workers was standing at the open doorway, staring at the flipchart before the training group came in. On it I had written a quote from a forgotten executive called Clarence Francis:

> You can buy a person's time; you can buy their physical presence at a given place; you can even buy a measured number of skilled muscular motions per hour. But you cannot buy loyalty. You cannot buy the devotion of hearts, minds or souls. You must earn these.

To this quote I had added, "These things the average person is ready to give freely, in return for evidence that they personally count and that the job they do is appreciated."

The factory guy strode in, jabbed the flipchart and said, quite emotionally, "Can I have a copy of that? Can you make them all write that down and remember it?"

People have a very basic desire for recognition and attention. It's obvious in kids, but the need is just as present in adults.

How much is enough? The need varies but there's no one working for you who likes being ignored, especially when they know, and you know, that they're doing a good job.

A simple thank you and a comment about good work done will be noticed by most people. The absence of it is keenly felt.

To understand how important the need for feedback and recognition is, a boss might do well to listen to people who leave well-paid, reasonably high-status roles:

I felt I wasn't getting anywhere.
I want to do something useful.
I'm not making a difference.
I'm just stuck in a rut and feel the need for a change.

When employees think there's no chance that they'll get recognition for positive things, they can leave, or they can go after attention for doing negative things. In everyday terms, they can become shit-stirrers, whiners and problem employees, purely for the attention.

People can feel resentful when they are finally told, after handing in their resignation, that they were highly valued and even being considered for promotion. "Why are they telling me this now?" is a fair question.

And exit interviews, carried out with apparent interest and concern, are just too little, too late. We ask people why they're leaving and the answer is, "I've found something else." The question we need to be asking is, "Why did you start looking?" And they may, justifiably, feel a lack of interest in answering that honestly. It doesn't matter. It's all too late.

WHERE DOES MONEY FIT IN TO MOTIVATION?

Of course money matters. Money is certainly an incentive but it's naive to think that people are only motivated by money.

If you offer $500 to anyone in the office who will do fifty push-ups, some people will get on the floor and start doing push-ups, some will look at you as if you're mad, some will start negotiating for more, or say it's not worth it. Others might say "Who do you think you are?" or "What do you think I am?" and still others could say "I can't. Physically, I can't."

Throw money at work performance and you get a similar range of reactions and nothing terribly predictable.

Ask almost any employee if they could earn more money elsewhere and the answer is invariably, and quite honestly, yes. They simply don't want the things that would go with the change. That might be longer hours, a longer commute, a move to another place, or some other exchange for the money that's simply not worth it to them.

Other motivating factors mean a great deal. People will jump ship to follow a manager who has inspired them. Entire teams can leave overnight. When that happens, it has very little to do with money.

We all need money but we have such different ideas of enough. For some people money spells status, for others it's a cure for their insecurities, and for others it represents love, or compensation for the lack of it. Consider the way that families fall out over wills. If you've seen people come close to a war over a dinner set then you might have already figured that you're never going to pay some people enough and keep everyone happy. And happiness is, as we know, not the point anyway. You can be happy and not necessarily very effective at work.

A manager from a company with very high staff turnover disagreed that money was not the primary driver. "My guys head down the road for anyone that waves an extra fifty cents an hour at them." I'm sure that was true for him. Listening to the way he talked about his employees I'd have walked down the road for the same money or even a bit less. If people cannot see any difference between suppliers, then price becomes the only factor. If the burgers all taste the same, I might as well buy the cheapest. If the airlines are all giving poor service and squashing me in like a sardine then why not chase the cheapest ticket? If an employer does not stand out in any way, then I might as well make a straight financial decision. In industries where there is little difference between one gang and another, and there's the same low morale on any site and no loyalty to staff, then employees will probably "walk down the road for an extra fifty cents." So would anyone.

But even when someone is complaining about money, I'd argue there are probably other things going on, and that just fixing the pay gap will not make the problem go away. If you keep throwing money at the challenge of motivation and pay no heed to the other needs that people have, you'll require a very large wallet and you may only attract mercenary people.

Early in my career I had the task of putting pay rise notices on desks and into hands. I think they were appreciated for about ten seconds on average. "About time too" was a fairly common response. "When's the next one?" was another frequent response.

Interestingly, some managers will insist that the people who report to them are just there for the money, but will describe themselves as needing a sense of achievement and freedom to make decisions. This assumption repeats itself as you talk to different layers of management. This is a vicious circle. The people on the frontline doing the more labor-intensive work can then insist that the directors at the very top of large companies are purely concerned with feathering their own nests, whereas they truly care about the job. We can all make false assumptions about people, and until we talk to each other as equals in the workplace, those kinds of prejudices are bound to stay. The "money is the only motivator" myth will remain if we cling to dismal views about the needs and drivers of other human beings.

WHERE DOES SECURITY FIT IN TO MOTIVATION?

People can vary widely in their needs for recognition and money. They also vary in their need for security in employment.

Are you in any position to offer someone job security? It's not something many bosses can guarantee anymore. In fact, managers probably have the lowest assurances of job security.

The attractiveness of employees who stay long term has changed. The desire to work in large organizations that can offer a career for life has waned. Bosses once valued CVs that showed stability and a commitment to one place; today they'll barely question a year off spent backpacking or a complete career switch. Moving about in the workforce is no longer seen as a liability. Indeed, more progressive employers will see an employee with a potentially useful blend of skills and experiences.

With the demise of jobs for life, most of us have realized that we need to manage our own careers. I don't know many who have escaped redundancies or lay-offs in their working lives, or at least felt the breeze from a swinging axe through their organizations. What is interesting to me, is how blasé some people have become, and far from worrying about being made redundant actually plan ahead to ask for a payout when it's offered.

The actor Sir Michael Gambon once said, "I'm of the generation that's frightened not to take the jobs that are offered."

Where once a generation was afraid of losing work a younger employee today can be more afraid of staying somewhere too long. Where people once asked only job-related questions at interviews – if they asked a question at all – younger interviewees may lean forward and ask whether the job leaves time for their voluntary work or some other interest.

A big drawcard today is flexibility. Employees are increasingly attracted to places that will develop their skills and make their CV look good. Younger employees are less afraid to take time out, and I hear employees in every age group making conscious decisions about the work-life balance.

Don't worry that you can't offer job security. Few people still think it exists, unless they are very naive. The employees that you most want to keep are not assuming a job for life. They know that their only job security rests with their skills, experience, and the results they continue to achieve.

WHERE DOES FEAR FIT IN TO MOTIVATION?

If you pointed a gun at my head and ordered me to do something, I'd probably do it. I wouldn't do it willingly or happily. I certainly wouldn't do anything extra that I didn't have to do. I'd cooperate out of fear for my life. If there was any way I could run, I would. If there was a chance to get that gun off you, I would take it. I'd do as you said, but only for as long as you had that power over me. But you'd have to watch over me or have some kind of back-up force in place, because the minute I could defy you, I would.

I have not been motivated in this scenario, I've been coerced. It's not the same. There's a big difference between coercion and motivation.

A smart boss is always aiming to get employees to work at their best, as independently and capably as possible. Managing people with threats and negative feedback invariably results in sabotage. If people find ways to get their own back or take revenge, they will. It also means that a boss must become an overseer in the broadest sense. There is no time to effectively plan, lead and organize, you're too busy watching as a way of controlling.

Why would shouting, abuse or aggression ever be an effective motivator? How would these habits ever be likely to win someone's genuine commitment and enthusiasm?

INDOCTRINATION AND DIGNITY

Responsibility rests with the boss as a leader, to ensure that people work in a dignified work environment. That's not just about the way that you treat people personally, but how you protect them from the bullying, aggression and cruelty that employees might inflict on each other.

It's impossible to create a truly motivating work climate if people have to struggle to maintain their dignity or fail to treat each other with respect while at work. But a boss has to know what is inappropriate and what is happening before they can act upon it. What if the boss is a prime offender?

I have asked groups in the past if anyone has worked for a manager that spoke down to them, belittled them or ignored them.

Follow-up questions included: How did that impact your motivation? Did you want to do well? Did you want to come up with ideas? Did you feel like going the extra mile for that boss? How did it feel coming into work each day?

Comments fly in about doing the minimum required, and the varieties of sabotage are endless and quite clever.

Converse questions include: Did you ever work for someone who spoke to you as an adult, using good manners and respect? How did that impact your self-motivation? How did you feel coming into work?

Think about your own situation and work experiences. I'm sure you can obviously see how the behavior of the person you immediately report to impacts on your level of enthusiasm and energy, yet still I hear bosses say "I have no influence on morale because I have no control over the payroll."

Of course, morale and motivation are not the same, but there are sound reasons to treat each other with dignity in the workplace, even if we don't feel any moral obligation.

Abuse and bullying

I booked a ticket to hear an expert on leadership but I arrived at the venue too early so I camped in the very back of the hotel ballroom to read the paper in peace. The hotel staff were busy setting up the room. No one noticed me. Mr. Leadership Expert suddenly walked into the room looking angry and headed straight for a young hotel employee who was busy arranging the flipchart stands at the front. He pointed a finger into the young man's chest and shouted, "I told your people that I wanted five f***ing flipcharts in a semicircle. Five! Do you understand? Are you deaf or are you just plain stupid? Do you know what a semicircle is? When I say I want something done, I expect it to be done!"

The young guy mumbled an apology that I couldn't quite hear, but even from a distance I could see he had turned bright red. Mr. Leadership Expert, still at full volume, continued, "I am going to make more money today than you will make this year." He then stormed out of the room and his flipcharts were grudgingly put into a semicircle. I suspect the young employee harbored thoughts of placing those flipcharts in another kind of circle entirely.

Mr. Leadership Expert was indeed going to earn a fortune that day and I'm told he still does. I have met many bosses and foremen who could explain the basics of motivation and leadership to this man. Why be so cruel, rude and ultimately stupid? He needed the support of the hotel staff that day and he'd just done his best to ensure that they would sabotage him in some way.

> *Immodest words admit of no defense*
> *For want of decency is want of sense.*
> Roscommon

Abuse and bullying mixed with prejudice

When someone has carried a deep-seated prejudice all their lives, it's hard for them to stand back and say, "Gosh! It may be that my thinking is all wrong." Their belief has been protected in their mind for a long time. It has been fed and watered on a daily basis. It is a lens through which they view the world. They may counter arguments with "I'm not prejudiced! I'm just saying, that's the way the world is."

Prejudice that results in abuse erodes morale and whittles it down into anger. In too many workplaces, employees endure sexual harassment, bullying, intimidation, and even physical abuse. Some of the more recent and newsworthy cases have been defended in court as the offenders just having a joke, or that it was part of the company culture.

The kind of abuse we can dish out is not just from boss to employee, but between employees, and towards managers too. Irrelevant and just plain nasty comments about dress, appearance, age, sexual preferences, where we live, our funny surname, height, weight, hair – or lack of it – race and religion, or even hobbies, can all be up for attack.

I once worked in a company where I was seated near two people who came from extremely different backgrounds and religious beliefs. One colleague, I'll call him Ted, made many bigoted remarks to our female colleague, Cassandra, about her Buddhist religion and her race, and the fact that she'd had children with a man of European descent. Ted's religion was strongly against what he still referred to as mixed marriages. I find myself wincing even now at the extreme nature of these comments. Ted also made remarks about other staff, including myself, that were racist, sexist or just plain insulting. When I've repeated some of Ted's comments in training programs – simply to illustrate the worst kinds of things that can be said at work – people have been genuinely shocked and asked how he survived.

It's an excellent question and there were at least three reasons why Ted survived.

First, Cassandra was a Buddhist, and a model of patience. She never fought back or complained.

Second, I didn't do enough. I gave Ted the evil eye, but that was pointless. I complained to our manager, but that was pointless as well. I gave support to Cassandra but that was a Band-Aid approach. I believed that as long as Ted stayed in the role he had, then he couldn't do much damage. I couldn't have been more deluded.

Third, and I think most important, Ted survived because the company tolerated racism, sexism, bullying and harassment on a much wider scale. His comments were not endorsed by any written policy, or openly encouraged. No one agreed that his behavior was OK but it wasn't seen as an issue either. Had my Buddhist colleague spoken up about his behavior, her protest, however mild, would have been viewed as a nuisance. She would have been labeled as the problem person.

About six months after I left that department, I heard that Ted had been promoted. He was not qualified for the promotion, nor able to perform the role. He'd be interviewing people and providing advice on issues such as inappropriate behavior. I was horrified and rang our former boss. "Oh give the guy a break," he said, "he's got a wife and kid to support."

The company continued to promote other guys just like Ted. It disproportionately rewarded anyone who fit the white male, Anglo-Saxon profile and did an excellent job of excluding those who did not. This was not written policy and would never have been admitted to, but it existed and was very strong. Managers hung onto rituals that protected their right to be aggressive, exclusive and insulting, while insisting on respect for themselves.

The worst of the bullies denigrated any attempt to improve their people skills or develop business acumen. Yet perversely they insisted that it was a people business that only they, with their unique insight into human beings, could understand and manage. If asked how we should develop the next generation of managers, many would insist that such skills could not be taught because you had to be born with the ability, and coincidentally, they just happened to be blessed in that respect.

Sexism and bullying were common, barely noticed by many and defended as "cultural" by others. Men demanded that they be addressed as "Mr." while women were always called by their first names, or collectively "the girls", or nothing at all. Older men felt it was their right to shout at and bully younger male staff on an apprenticeship scheme and tearing a strip off someone in public was not unusual.

The curious thing is that I look back at those days with a lot of fond memories too. Aside from the Teds I had to deal with, I met some wonderful people and had a great time. But if I'd stayed there another five years, how would I ever have escaped the indoctrination? The next company I worked for had a similarly powerful culture, but it was entirely composed of the opposing values and behaviors.

It's very hard to get through to some managers and leaders that their offensiveness and bigotry is inconsistent with their belief that they're a good boss.

> *When a stupid man is doing something he is ashamed of, he always declares that it is his duty.*
>
> George Bernard Shaw

Many of us learn to shrug off bad behavior and carry on. We trot out excuses such as "I can handle it" or "Didn't do me any harm." But it most certainly does do us harm to turn a blind eye to abuse, bullying and discrimination. It teaches us to lower our standards and to accept the unacceptable.

When we see managers doing nothing about bullying and abuse, or even promoting the worst offenders, it teaches us that it's OK. Those with ambition may take on the coldness and insensitivity of those they want to replace. Those on the receiving end may block out their feelings and try to stop listening. That will affect their ability to work and will certainly pull down morale. Lowering the standards of decency and accepting undignified behavior can also erode confidence, loyalty and the general belief that employers are fair and professional. Behavior breeds behavior, so it's not hard to imagine that others might think that if management can't be fair and professional, then why should I?

Useful guidelines on bullying and harassment advise us to protect employees from:

- spreading of malicious rumors or insults.
- memos or emails that criticize a person and start circulating around the workplace.
- ridicule.
- being picked on, teased or constantly criticized.
- being set up to fail.
- exclusion or victimization.
- overbearing supervision or abuses of power.
- unwelcome sexual advances – and that includes standing too close or allowing pornographic material to be on display in the workplace.

A smart boss doesn't need the hovering stick of the law to instill protection against this behavior. Basic decency and respect between people is a healthy thing for any workplace to aspire to. Maintaining a reasonably polite and humane environment is a morale booster. Stand back and question how things could be. A good boss will try to lift the standards of behavior and aim to uphold a mutually respectful workplace.

We don't choose the people we work with. We don't have to love them or even like them. They will have views and thoughts that we disagree with. But we do, as managers, have to watch out for abuse and undignified behavior between workers. Good managers stand up to abuse, bullying and harassment and treat them as unacceptable no matter who is the target.

CHAPTER SEVEN

LETTING PEOPLE GO

**WHAT TO DO WHEN AN EMPLOYEE LEAVES YOU
WHAT TO DO WHEN YOU ARE ENDING THE
CONTRACT**

*

> *When I was sixteen I worked in a pet store.*
> *And they fired me because they had three*
> *snakes in there and one day I braided them.*
> *Steve Wright, comedian*

I'm writing this book to cover just about any type of business
in any country but it is important to note that, particularly
with this subject, employment laws change and employees
are covered by vastly different rules and policies. The advice
is very general so please get up-to-the-minute legal advice.
From the giving of references to dealing with abandoned

employment, you should observe contracts and your own policies at a minimum. This reduces the likelihood of grievance actions and helps you to stay out of courts and tribunals. It also shows that you are a fair boss and that's a very handy reputation to have.

WHAT TO DO WHEN AN EMPLOYEE LEAVES YOU

It's entirely normal for people to resign from a job and move on. Anyone can feel the need for a change, a new career or a move elsewhere. Some of us want or need to stay home with kids, retire, go back to study, travel, or set up a business. Sometimes life forces a change. Downshifting is more common today as people swap full-time, higher paid work, for less stress, more free time and fewer days commuting.

There's not a lot you can do to stop some resignations. You should, however, always talk with a good employee who is leaving you for a similar job elsewhere. If they were unhappy and there was a fair reason for it, is there anything to be learned from this? The fact that they've taken the initiative to look for something else, rather than stay and feel bored, angry or thwarted, is a good thing. The last thing you want is someone quitting mentally but staying on in the job. Those who whine for years that they hate their job or their employer are a pain, and sometimes need to be told that the security system is there to stop people from breaking in, not to prevent them from breaking out.

If a good employee resigns to go to someone who will pay them more, consider whether you are paying market values. If you're paying too low they won't be the first employee to leave. If the departing employee was highly valued, you might consider offering to match their new salary, or even increasing it in order to get them to stay – but think carefully before you rush into that kind of pledge. What message do you send to the rest of your staff if people have to resign to get the salary they were due? You might decide it's wiser to wish the person well and say goodbye. They may have moved on anyway in the emotional sense. People rarely leave jobs just for a small pay rise. Usually there are other factors at play. Money is a motivator, but it's rarely the only reason.

If the employee is moving on because there's an opportunity that you can't provide, then don't take that as a personal rejection. It's a good sign that people developed while they worked for you and felt confident to go onwards and upwards. Stay in touch with good employees if you can. And remember that every time someone leaves a workplace it creates an opportunity. It provides a smart manager with the chance to rethink and re-organize. It provides another employee with aspirations a chance to move up.

What to say when an employee tells you they're leaving

Ideally you should try to take the news calmly, wish them well, and then sort out the details. Try to look pleased for them, and avoid ranting and raving that they're deserting you or letting you down at a really bad time. They're not married to you.

If you want to say they'll be missed, then say that. It's normal to feel sorry if you're losing a good person. If you've been having problems with them, wait until you're in private before you jump up and down crying "Yippee!"

There is some planning to be done. What date do they wish to finish up? How does this match the notice period in their contract? When the date is agreed, put a handover plan in place.

Acknowledge the time and contribution the leaving employee has made to your business and try to part on the best possible terms. You could make a simple speech, host a farewell drink, hand them a bunch of flowers, a cake or a card from everyone. It doesn't have to be a formally organized event – but do something. A selfish reason for this is that the person remains a promoter of your business and a contact for the future. Even retrenchments and redundancies can be handled in a dignified manner that allows the person to end their employment with you in a reasonable way. People remember their starts and finishes with employers.

Another good reason why you should behave with decency is the signal it sends to the people who remain with you. They are watching to see how their contributions will be finally acknowledged, and there can be a great deal of resentment at the way a valued and longstanding colleague was treated if it wasn't done right.

Security and Handovers

What is your normal procedure with regard to security? Are there issues around keys, passes, codes, laptops, credit cards, information, clients, public relations and so on to consider? Sometimes companies walk the departing employee to the door. This is usually done politely and not by the scruff of the neck. Employees who have full access to systems, sensitive financial data or customer information are sometimes escorted out. This is to prevent them giving this information to a competitor. It's a fairly pointless exercise. If the person was planning to leave they've had plenty of time to copy files and even keys. Anyway, you can't erase files in their head. Sometimes you just have to trust people. There are other ways to ensure ongoing security and this might be better served by including clauses in their contracts.

References

You're not compelled to write a character reference, but if you agree to provide one then write it carefully. A character reference can be very helpful for someone's future and if you think highly of this person and would not hesitate to recommend them, then say so.

But please, do not write a glowing reference for someone you've just fired. It dilutes the value of honest references and turns you into a hypocrite. Some managers get caught in the trap of wanting to be helpful when they've let someone go. You may end up answering a tribunal as to why you fired someone you clearly thought was terrific.

You can always write a certificate of service, which is a factual statement that gives the dates of joining and leaving, the position or title held, a brief description of duties and a reason for leaving.

If someone resigns and then appears to stop working, then it's wise to bring their employment to a rapid conclusion.

Burning Bridges

Sometimes employees don't handle leaving very well. If they become highly offensive or do something stupid, like launching into a bitter tirade in a farewell speech, then stay calm and rise above it. Don't respond to the offensive comments, it isn't worth it. You needn't burn the bridge either.

If you really can't stand the person, you won't have to see them again so there's no need for parting shots.

An associate of mine was disappointed but supportive when his employee wanted to leave and set up his own business. When the company laptop was grudgingly returned, he found months' worth of evidence that the protégé had been attempting to take clients with him.

> "When I realized I'd been paying his salary while he'd been doing this, I was shocked and hurt. He'd started out with me as a graduate and it was a kick in the teeth. I asked him directly about these emails and got a load of abuse about my right to have the laptop back at all. It was such a stupid way to end things. If he'd done it right, I'd have been able to send him some work to get started. Now I'll make sure it always goes to someone else."

If they destroy or pinch property, sabotage equipment, or demand something they're not entitled to, then consider what level of action is justified. You may feel differently about a serious embezzlement than you do about missing highlighter pens.

When someone leaves by just not showing up

Formal notice may not be a priority in some workplaces with high turnover and casual labor. However, if you think that a sudden absence is unusual for an employee, don't leap to negative conclusions. Take a lesson from a colleague of mine, who was instructed to send a missing employee a dismissal letter. He argued that this didn't seem right and asked permission to visit the man's home. After looking through windows and noticing that things didn't look right, he found the employee had died at home alone. Imagine the grieving family opening that terse dismissal note with your business letterhead and name on it.

If you're confident that the person has simply left with no intention of returning then obviously the contract has ended through their actions and they are effectively dismissed.

What to do if someone leaves through serious injury, sickness or death

Typically larger workplaces have some plan in place for handling death and injury in the workplace. This would include communicating with the relatives and their communities. In large companies, there's usually a Health and Safety officer to refer to or a senior HR person. They would be expecting, as part of their role, to step in and handle deaths, traumas and injuries. Your first course of action is to consult with those people.

However, if you're a boss in a small- or medium-sized workplace, then you might find yourself having to make some rapid and tactful decisions.

In the case of injury or illness, once the person is in hospital or at home recovering, then discreet monitoring of the situation is needed. Obviously you can't hover in an intensive care unit and complain that their work is piling up or you may appear a wee bit callous. Are they going to be able to come back to work at all, or is this an insurance case requiring assistance with lawyers, administrators and so on?

Colleagues will want to know what's happening and it's helpful if the person is not deluged with visits, so try to appoint someone to act as the communications link, if you're not the obvious link.

Hopefully you'll never have to handle someone dying at work – but it does happen. You will have to deal with some kind of inquiry if this was a workplace accident. As a general rule, an autopsy is required when a person dies in any unusual circumstance, and suddenly dying at work is invariably unusual. In an ideal world you'll have a system in place, but if you don't, you must consult with your most senior managers or the relevant legal bodies in health and safety.

If anyone witnesses a death or injury then it's likely they're suffering a degree of distress. Is there any support or counseling that might be offered for those who were involved?

A colleague can seem, and indeed be, perfectly well one moment and gone the next. Extreme diplomacy is required. Employees who worked with this person are going to have some reaction. If you notice that some employees are struggling with shock then seek some advice or counseling for them.

Obviously the greatest tact is called for when dealing with a grieving family. Is there anything you can do to assist in dealing with pension companies, insurers, helping to swiftly process final payments, and any other details a bereaved family should not have to cope with? Give them some days of privacy before going to visit, and if they're not ready to see you just yet, or even angry and feeling inclined to take it out on someone, then you have to understand that.

People are remarkably resilient, even when a death has come as a huge shock, but a wise move is to close down the workplace or unit for at least one day, if you can. Your customers and the public will understand this, unless you work in an essential service.

What do your remaining employees wish to do for this person or their family? Just ask them. Do they want to send flowers or some other tribute? Do colleagues wish to attend a memorial service or the funeral? The person's immediate managers should attend. If you're inexperienced in such situations, then call in a more experienced employee or manager to help. That is far better than getting it wrong.

WHAT TO DO WHEN YOU ARE ENDING THE CONTRACT

Dismissal for gross misconduct or summary dismissal

I often hear bosses insist that you can't fire people these days. I think this comes from believing that because they're not free to dismiss someone on a whim then they can't let them go at all. But people are let go from their places of employment every day – sometimes fairly and sometimes unfairly. Some of those cases get to a court or tribunal but many do not.

Employment laws may not cover all your employees. Many employees accept being dismissed (even unfair dismissal) and never make a claim.

There are industries and workplaces where militant unions follow up a justifiable dismissal or even a deserved warning by some industrial action or threat of it. There are frivolous claims and biased tribunals that stick in many people's minds and I have seen my share.

But the idea that the system will always block you is only a perception. In fact union reps can be surprisingly supportive on issues like health and safety.

Union membership is not, and should never be, protection against having to do your job, or exemption from the obvious rules. The better and more responsible union reps are usually keen to see that a fair and reasonable process is followed. A good manager will understand that and support it.

What may lie behind the belief that you can't sack anyone is a reluctance to follow the proper process, or the belief that the process is so difficult you may as well not bother. I've had managers demand that I fire an employee who has been a problem for "years" when they haven't issued a single warning, or had any sort of performance review to discuss the pressing issues. In some cases they have consistently given them pay rises.

Sometimes I think this excuse is held onto because the manager is avoiding discomfort and conflict. It's stressful to do these things but it is a part of being a professional manager.

And why should we be able to fire someone easily? Severing income and employment is a drastic thing to do. Being dismissed from a job can haunt a person and hurt their reputation for life. The experience can be traumatic. There are plenty of documented examples of employees doing harm to themselves or others as a result of being fired. A reasonable and fair process is not that difficult to apply, and pretty logical if you consider what you would want for yourself.

Gross misconduct, on the other hand, is an action that usually justifies immediate dismissal. Ordinarily you would not need to go through warnings or discussions or worry about writing references, but you should be very sure of your facts before you instantly dismiss an employee. Would you like to be fired in the next ten minutes on hearsay or suspicion?

The actions that usually constitute gross misconduct and instant termination of a contract can include stealing, embezzlement or fraud, serious breaches of health and safety, gross insubordination (which can include refusing to act upon a reasonable request), failing a drug and alcohol test, assaulting another employee, intoxication, or anything you may specifically have in your workplace policy.

Dismissal for performance

You can reasonably dismiss an employee for:

- Conduct – their behavior is not acceptable. For example, they are rude and unhelpful to your customers.
- Capability or qualification – they cannot do their job or continue to do their job. For example, they need a driver's license and they've been disqualified from driving, or they're falling below the required work standards.
- Any substantial reason: you can let someone go for anything you believe is fair and reasonable, but be ready to explain in the clearest terms what the problem is and why it's a problem. If you believe you have a justifiable and fair reason to give someone a warning then go ahead, but proceed on the basis that there is a definite and observable gap between what the employee is paid to do and what they are routinely doing.

You need to be very honest with yourself. Are you just desperate to be rid of this person because you can't stand them? Are they doing their job but just doing exactly what they have to do and no more? Are you threatened by this person because they're good or because you think they might take your job one day? Are you jealous of them? It happens. There are managers who sit on, thwart, or try to ditch their best employees. It sounds daft but anyone who has worked for an insecure manager or a control freak will have seen this. Many human resources staff will have come across the manager who demands an employee be fired when there's no justifiable reason for this action and it will not stand up in a court of law, if it gets to one. Look closely at the background stories of the more recent corporate disasters and major frauds, and you can usually find someone in the story who was fired or disciplined for speaking up – and quite likely labeled as "difficult" before their last day there.

> *He shows great originality which must be curbed at all costs.*
> *From an early school report of Peter Ustinov, who was an Oscar-winning actor and Ambassador for UNICEF, among other accomplishments.*

The Discipline Process – trying to get someone back on track

In the case of performance gaps you should approach the first stage with the aim of getting the person back on track. Be prepared to hear of circumstances that may change your perception entirely – from ill health to personal problems, to being let down by colleagues, system failures or genuine resource shortages. Stay open-minded and consider the first conversation an exploratory meeting between adults.

How do employees normally figure out what they're supposed to be doing in your workplace?

If your answer is "Well, they're big enough, aren't they? They ought to know!" then think about whether it's fair to leave people to guess the results or standards that are expected. An employee might not know exactly what you want or don't want. It's also possible that they're following a bad example picked up elsewhere.

Some questions that need answers:

- Could you solve the situation by explaining again, clearly and carefully, exactly what they should be doing and what is expected?
- Do they know why their behavior is a problem and what they ought to be doing instead?
- Was the person coached, trained, or instructed to work in a certain way that was wrong?
- Is their contract clear?
- Have there been other means of telling them what to do, such as briefings, toolbox talks, noticeboards, memos, emails, or other kinds of messages that spell things out very clearly?
- Have you already clarified this situation? Has a warning already been issued?

It's entirely possible that you might resolve this problem early on with some retraining or re-explaining.

You need to look at what a person is achieving and then at the person directly. An extremely talented and capable person may have results that are below par. So first check the facts and make absolutely sure that it is their performance that's below standard.

This information could come from:

- a gap in the results required.
- a loss of business.
- complaints from others such as employees or customers.
- missed deadlines.

- systems or machinery that is working correctly.
- increased levels of damage, problems or faults.
- your own observation.

Be very clear about these facts before you proceed. An employee may refute the evidence point blank, even when it comes to timekeeping and the security cameras prove it, or you have directly observed them walking in late for ten days in a row. I've seen people dig their heels in and insist "No I wasn't. Your watch is wrong, and all these office clocks are wrong."

If you find the idea of being prepared to discuss a serious issue with an employee to be too daunting and best "left alone" then it could be a good time to review your performance as a manager. Clear information about an employee's performance should be easy to obtain if you're planning, organizing and controlling work with any sort of system at all. If you don't know exactly what's going on, you'll be on very thin ice telling an employee that they have a performance problem.

Once you're very clear of your facts on performance or results then consider the person. Now you're looking at willingness and capability.

1. Are they willing but not able?
2. Are they able but not willing?
3. Are they unwilling and unable?
4. Are they willing and able?

I've known bosses whose immediate response to all performance issues is "Sack 'em!"

I've known other bosses whose answer to every work problem is a nice talk or a chat over a beer, which they repeat for years with the same problem and the same person, slowly despairing that they've tried hard but the problem isn't shifting. I wonder why?

And there are managers whose reaction to all four possibilities is to hide and just hope it will all go away.

But depending on where you place this person, you might proceed differently.

1. If they are willing but unable then you have a skills shortfall. You might consider whether you're prepared to train, coach, or have the person closely supervised until they are up to standard. It's good to have employees who are willing. Don't rush in to dismiss them too quickly if you think they're worth the time to train. Is it possible your systems changed so much that a willing employee who was once able is now struggling? Is there a hidden illness, stress or increasing disability? Hint: I've seen more than a few employees in denial about loss of hearing or problematic eyesight.

You need to talk to these employees about how to get back up to speed, or agree to some other resolution.

2. Are they able but not willing? A person who is able but not willing is probably having some kind of motivation problem. Talk to them about what's going on. People always have reasons for the things they do. Are they cheesed off about something at work? Is there a problem at home? Are they well? Whatever it is, talk it through, offer support and decide what you want to do after agreeing to move forward. If they won't tell you, you can't force the issue but they can't go on endlessly with under par results and a willingness issue.

My friend Tom is a manager in a large and well-known professional company. He tells me "almost every time we face this able but unwilling problem, it uncovers a family member who's ill or some personal trauma that the employee is trying to cope with while doing their job. Once the situation is clear it gives us the chance to shift the work around and help support the person for a while. We can often refer them to counseling or some other help. In almost all these conversations the employee knows they're not up to speed and they feel relieved to finally talk about what's happening."

If it's a terminal loss of interest or commitment, then it's still a good opportunity to address the situation because it can't continue. The employee is likely to be aware that they're not performing and it may force a resolution one way or another.

3. Are they willing and able? You might wonder how someone can be willing and able, but be underperforming. It doesn't sound possible but it can happen for many reasons.

- Perhaps their part of the business is still growing or developing.
- Perhaps their machinery is letting them down.
- They might be genuinely under-resourced.
- They might be in a research phase of development that requires patience in terms of positive results.
- They might be working on a project or part of the business that is a loss leader or simply cannot win.
- The market might be against them, for example, selling ice cream in winter.
- Their product may now be superseded by the competition.
- They might be a trainee who's not completely performing at full speed yet.

This poor performer might help you improve your business because their problem may show you a system failure. A good boss would want to get to the cause of that and fix it.

In this case, the person is not the problem so rushing in to dismiss, counsel or train someone who's willing and able is not going to do anything but frustrate and demoralize. Willing and able people are pretty handy to have and if you don't want to manage them then your competitors might.

4. Are they unwilling and unable?

Why have you got an employee who is unwilling and unable and underperforming? How long are you going to carry this person? What has happened to your standards of finding people and controlling work?

Don't faff around forever with the unable and unwilling employees of the world unless you love the word bankruptcy and you're happy to annoy your other workers.

Get involved in your recruitment to ensure you're not employing the unwilling and unable if this is a situation you're facing too often with new starters.

Tips for having a constructive disciplinary talk

People can usually handle difficult feedback and bad news if you keep it constructive and relevant. (But see the next section about how it can go pear-shaped for the times when it doesn't go well.)

Try not to approach the conversation as if you're going into battle. If you worry too much about controlling the situation or winning, then you may find yourself getting caught up in a mini power struggle. Useful tips before you start:

- Make sure your talk will be private.
- Keep notes, or have someone there to take notes. It's wise in most circumstances for the boss to have a witness, and certainly a good idea to take notes.

- Let them have someone with them, particularly for final warnings or dismissals. There are workplaces where you must allow that.
- Assume that the person wants to change things for the better. It's not always true. Sometimes people don't give a toss and behave accordingly, but assuming the best in people will give you a more professional tone of voice and demeanor, which is likely to help.
- Keep saying to yourself, "I'm doing this to help the situation turn around" because at the very least, that will calm you and probably keep the conversation on an adult level.
- Then stay calm.

And once you start:

- Tell the employee about your concerns and give them the relevant facts.
- Don't talk down to them as if they've been naughty or stupid.
- Don't grovel to them either, as if you're so very, very sorry you have to do this mean and horrible thing.
- Give them time to take this in.
- Don't make any comments about their personality or attitude.
- Don't jump to any conclusions about why their performance is down.
- Let them offer their reasons and listen – even if you think it sounds unacceptable.
- Don't get sidetracked.
- Be clear about what you expect instead.
- Talk about moving forward as if it's a joint decision.

- Agree a plan to move forward.
- Make a time in the near future for a review.

It may catch you by surprise when an employee is fully aware that things aren't right. People's honesty about their own conduct can be an eye-opener.

Choose your words very carefully. They can be used against you in a tribunal so think before you speak, and if necessary hold back from commenting or adjourn the meeting.

The employee is not going to leave your office laughing and doing the can-can, but if you have focused on the future and talked as if you want to see change for the better, then it's likely they will reflect on the conversation as a show of decency and an opportunity to get it together.

Remember you're doing this in order to improve performance and get them back on track. Just keep in mind how you would like to be treated and spoken to if you were on the receiving end and you'll probably do well.

Coping when the conversation goes pear-shaped

It can be hard work telling someone what they need to hear, when they can always find others to tell them what they want to hear. Some people have appalling insight into their behavior and a deeply exaggerated sense of their accomplishments. This is why you need facts. They are your only defense against the employee in denial.

It's not unheard of for someone to behave badly or become hyper-defensive. Don't get sidetracked by difficult behavior, antagonism or threats. If the person becomes abusive or insulting then that in itself gives rise to disciplinary action. You are a manager and you have every right to manage performance.

Don't get thrown by sarcastic remarks that are designed to wound, such as, "This is just typical of people like you. You think you're so high and mighty." Don't get caught up in a Yes you did/No I didn't back and forth or some argument over a side issue. Don't put up with a history lesson about the strike of 1923 when this problem started. Listen, but then move it on.

You may get some irrelevant objections thrown back at you. "I'm still paying off my car" is not relevant. If the last boss never said anything, again that is not relevant. It's not relevant that "Peter does the same thing." It's easy to get distracted but you must get the conversation back on topic.

On the other hand, the employee might accept every word you say and suddenly realize that they're in a bit of trouble. If it has come as a shock and the person is distressed, give them time to compose themselves. Have tissues handy. If it becomes impossibly emotional, then call an adjournment and agree to a later time that day if possible.

Always stop the conversation if something comes to light that changes the facts completely, as long as the new facts are directly relevant to the issue.

Write up your notes immediately. Even if your process does not require you to record the conversation, do it anyway. Call it a record of meeting or an aide memoire.

Be seen to be fair and reasonable

A lot of people will turn their performance or behavior around but what if the situation does not get better?

If this is the case then you're going to have to continue with your process of dismissal and ultimately let the person go. A fair process usually consists of a warning, a final warning, and then dismissal. Even if the process only required a first verbal warning, it would still be wise to make a record of that conversation. Obviously these warnings are spaced apart, but not too far apart. They should be far enough apart so that the person has a reasonable chance to demonstrate an improvement.

Tribunals (if it goes that far) may want to establish whether the employee had fair warning, a chance to argue their case, and was kept informed about what was going on. They might want to know whether there were unreasonable delays or whether the issues were set down clearly for the employee. Was the time and place of meetings agreed to with the employee? These requirements are only reasonable, and a good guide to behaving with decency in any case. Once again, ask yourself – what would you hope for if it was you?

When you're writing a warning, make it brief and to the point – what happened and why. Be very concise. Once you're organized to warn or dismiss, get on with it as soon as possible. Keep the situation as confidential as possible. The employee may be talking to others in the workplace but you have to be discreet.

Don't drag the process out at any stage and please don't tell an employee a week in advance to come and see you "and bring a support person with you if you want." That is painful and unnecessary. You may even see tactical stress where the person feigns illness and takes sick leave for suspiciously extended periods in order to avoid the conversation. There are lawyers and friends who will advise an employee to do that and some doctors who will sign any sick leave note that their patients request. My favorite was a doctor's note signed "headache – five days."

Continuing to work with a person during the weeks of a disciplinary process is a real test of your leadership ability and good manners. Talk to friends and family for support because you won't get much warmth from work, and besides, you can only confide in peers, not the person's colleagues.

The stress of these situations explains why a lot of managers don't confront performance issues. They can't stand feeling like the bad guy. It's possible you may not get much help from HR either.

In larger companies there's usually an internal appeal process. Employees are also entitled to know what to do and who to speak to if they want to appeal. This is usually spelled out in policies and staff handbooks but you should remind the person. Some other manager who appears to be neutral can be appointed for an appeal if this occurs and you're in a larger workplace. In small businesses this is not possible.

Once you've decided to dismiss someone, put your decision and the reasons for it in writing so it can be handed to them on the spot.

Giving notice and the practicalities of firing someone

Being dismissed for non-performance or conduct should never come as a big shock. It's the final stage of a process where warnings should have already been given.

"Notice" is usually observed by those resigning rather than those dismissing but notice and final dismissal can be vague in the law. Never ignore your formal policies if you have them.

An overbearing manager I once worked with boasted that he wore a black shirt and black tie to work if he was firing someone. "And then everyone knows the minute I walk in that I mean business." This is management at its worst. He took an immature delight in having power over others in this situation. But this is not a time for gamesmanship. This is a time for being as decent as you can be, at the very least because you need to show your remaining staff how you behave in difficult circumstances.

The best day for letting someone go is a Monday. The second best day is a Tuesday. The worst day is a Friday and the worst time is late on a Friday.

On a Monday or Tuesday, the dismissed person can start making applications, visiting job agencies and even attending interviews. They may have a new job to go to by the end of the week.

On a Friday night, a dismissed person can do very few of these things. They may go out drinking and will do so in a pretty dismal frame of mind. There is a very long weekend ahead of them in which to worry and become angry. They may go home to a family and visit their anger and frustration upon them.

On a Monday you can also get everyone else at work together to announce the change, take some questions and then get the place settled down and moving forward.

On a Friday, the entire workplace has the weekend to (potentially) stew on it and wonder what happened. The rumor mill then has a two-day start on your communications.

Choose early in the week if you possibly can.

Being fired is still a blow and people may crumble. I can still see an ashen-faced older manager at the top of the stairs at a company I worked for a long time ago. I looked up thinking he was about to fall or have a heart attack. I knew what had happened and why he'd been instantly dismissed but I didn't have to attend the meeting.

You might offer to see a dismissed person home to their front door. Obviously you would organize that very quietly ahead of time with a sensible driver. If you can ask for the assistance of someone to escort (not frog-march) them out, then do so. Maybe you'll do this yourself but handle it calmly and with a bit of sympathy. Getting dismissed workers home safely serves another purpose – you're ensuring they're not wandering around the workplace. Be aware that badmouthing and destabilizing of other employees can occur, as can various forms of theft and sabotage.

Final pay must be consistent with their legal rights or whatever is in their contract and it would be wise to have any certificate of separation or letter confirming service, and check, cash or bank payment summary ready, depending on your usual practice.

It's possible you may soon face angry friends or relatives coming into the workplace. If you have security or a reception, warn them of any dismissals that have just occurred. It's often the case that the angry relative does not know the truth of the situation. It's not up to you to explain the details to them and you're not obliged to answer in any detail. It's also possible that the person who was just dismissed doesn't know they are there.

Do not hire a dismissed employee back in as a temp or contractor. I'm sure that sounds painfully obvious but I've seen bosses do it and then regret it. "We were really busy at the time" is the usual excuse.

And to repeat a point, do not write a glowing reference for someone you dismissed just because you feel guilty. A tribunal might naturally wonder why you say one thing and do another.

Unfair dismissal

When Henry Ford II fired Lee Iacocca, he explained, "I just don't like you."

If that was the only problem then that would be deemed to be an unfair dismissal.

Along with firing someone because you don't like them, you cannot fire people because:

- They asked for the minimum legislated wage, or basic rights to leave and pay, or equal pay. (They shouldn't have had to ask in the first place.)
- They are pregnant or on leave that was agreed.
- They are a union rep or rep of some workplace committee.
- Of their color, sex, sexual preference, religion or beliefs.
- They have raised a genuine problem or issue, particularly about something that is in the public interest. This is generally true in many countries now even if they're ultimately wrong.

However, no one is Teflon-coated just because they're pregnant, a union rep, or a member of a minority. No one is excused from meeting standards of performance or conduct. You shouldn't be afraid to tackle a genuine performance problem or gross misconduct situation just because someone throws the word discrimination at you.

Whistle-blowing is a relatively new area in employment law. Someone with a genuine concern for the business or an objection to the way something is being handled is not necessarily a troublemaker who needs to be dealt with. You cannot fire someone for trying to do what they believe is the right thing. They may be wrong but that doesn't make them a problem employee. Poor managers are easily threatened and made insecure by those who question them, but people who speak up are usually doing so because they care. Employees who really want you to suffer will sit back and let you make bad decisions.

Handling your own feelings

Dismissals produce the ingredients for very unpleasant moments. Good bosses never get used to firing people and nor should they. If you feel drained, upset, tired or saddened, these are very normal reactions. If you feel a bit angry with the person and think that it could all have been avoided if they had just done this or that differently, that's a normal reaction too.

The loss of employment is a very serious matter to an individual and must be approached with care. That's not to say you should fear what is necessary for your business and go to ridiculous lengths to avoid it, as many bosses can do.

Some of us can be so cowed by the person's union membership or perceived strength that we pick on smaller issues and easier targets and let the big fish swim by. It's certainly more difficult to sack someone who you see socially, or dismiss people who are considered part of the furniture. If they have relatives and friends in your workplace then that can cause concern. None of this justifies avoiding a genuine problem.

You may have to deal with the curled lip and sneer of the employee's friends but you should be able to handle that. There could be resignations in sympathy, although in my experience, they're usually welcome. There may well be the odd "Oh, but she was so nice" comment, but unfortunately niceness doesn't guarantee us job security if we're not up to scratch.

Usually the strongest reactions come from people who are also borderline discipline cases and realize it. There's obvious shock and self-preservation in those reactions. They're trying to warn you not to go after them too.

Don't be put off by empty threats. I was once visited by another manager, warning me that the dismissed employee would go to the local paper. "Make sure they spell my name right" is the answer to that one. Of course it never happened.

A colleague once had to dismiss an employee who had been caught stealing equipment over a period of time. He felt physically sick about having to do this, having known and liked the man. However, as a good manager he understood that any theft or fraud must warrant instant dismissal, if not prosecution. Within the hour he had been visited by employees who challenged him with "Didn't you think about his wife and kids?" My colleague countered with "Didn't he?"

We're not excused for gross misconduct or continued poor performance because we're married with children or because we're a nice person. You cannot let people get away with fraud or theft, breaches of health and safety, bullying, abuse, or any other acts that can destroy a business and morale, and are just plain wrong.

But you can also discover that other employees fully understand what you've done and feel encouraged that standards and conduct matters to the employer. There are few things more demoralizing than working alongside people who do not pull their weight or who drag the business down and get away with it.

Letting go of a "difficult" employee

Occasionally a boss will insist they have someone who is bullet-proof or untouchable. They will insist that this person cannot be let go. The staff will use phrases such as "getting away with murder" or "protected species."

Difficult long servers may have survived even when there was a chance to lose them in cutbacks. This is largely due to someone deciding that they're too expensive to pay off. This is short-sighted – they're too expensive to keep. What message is sent when an enthusiastic new starter is sacrificed for a notorious idler?

Difficult people can be quite predictable and persistent. Often their behavior seems quite hopelessly embedded. They got away with behaving badly while getting others to accept it by backing down. Wouldn't you keep doing something if it worked? It's worth saying that this might be their behavior at work and not necessarily typical of the person. (Perhaps they just don't get away with it at home.)

If you are planning to let this person go, then use exactly the same procedure as you would for any other performance issue. It's just another disciplinary situation.

Check your facts.

- Is this person's work under the standard required? Prove it.
- Were they clear about the standards expected? Check that.
- Is their behavior affecting the work performance of the team or people in it?
- What are they doing that's a problem? Answer specifically.
- How is it affecting work? Be prepared to answer specifically.
- What should they do instead?

This is all standard preparation for any disciplinary action. What *may* differ is that you want to cover yourself in a few extra layers. You may go to extra lengths to make sure things are witnessed and that the process is followed expertly with clear minutes and letters and/or emails to follow up conversations.

You should be precise with your documentation. But frankly, you should be this diligent with every dismissal.

Set some ground rules, stay calm and talk to the person as an equal professional. That's not easy if you approach them with trepidation or loathing. Just be clear, concise and fair.

Don't ever consider a tempting pay-off for a difficult employee. What would this do to the morale of your other employees? What message would it send about standards and values? What would it say about you – as a manager – if that was the way you chose to solve a performance problem? Indeed, it may indicate that you are the main performance problem, since your best solution for failing to manage someone is to throw money or some other reward at them. Please don't promote them.

What really makes someone "difficult?" How does someone earn this label? How is it that they don't qualify for gross misconduct?

Some examples that spring to mind are the individuals who:

- Threaten to sue every five minutes.
- Wave the words discrimination and bullying often to intimidate managers.
- Know some dirt and use the threat of telling all to behave with a sense of impunity.
- Are connected to someone important and remind everyone when necessary.

- Frequently use the phrase "they wouldn't dare touch me" so that others come to believe it.
- Constantly work to garner sympathy from others for some reason.
- Are chronic malingerers who feign sickness and get other benefits but have not been caught.
- Are belligerent employees who make their colleagues grovel for a favor in order to get work done.
- Perform work in a willfully slow and obstructive manner, but always do some task that is necessary.
- Could do something destructive because of the knowledge and skill they have.
- Threaten to go to the press.
- Have made people personally afraid for their safety.

These are not the kind of employees that you want working for you. Do not imagine that they are indispensable, even if they have created that myth around themselves. If you are concerned, then plan how to plug that skills gap before you head into a disciplinary situation. A question you might ask is how one person came to be almost indispensable? It's a poor way to plan and organize a business if you only have one person who can perform some critical function. What happens when they are on leave? What happens if they were hit by a bus tomorrow?

Be wary of managers who defend a difficult employee because "they've been here forever." Frequently you hear terms like loyal and long serving when these do not match the behavior of the person being discussed. How can someone be loyal and consistently belligerent at the same time? A person is not loyal because they have sat in the one chair for twenty years. Habitual whiners are not loyal, although they frequently remind you about their years of service. Collecting a pay check but doing precious little to earn it means they have long served themselves, not the business. Don't confuse the terms loyalty and long serving with good performance.

Letting people go is not much fun and it's not meant to be. It might make you unpopular temporarily, but it comes with the job. You have to learn to handle other people's reactions because support can be thin on the ground among other managers who would rather hide under a rock.

The general guidelines are usually fair and reasonable, but I have come across employers that have internal disciplinary processes that really are absurd. In one company, the procedure for dismissing an employee was clearly written by someone in human resources who was worried about losing their job. They had made the process so long, so cumbersome, and so weighted in the employee's favor, that some managers looked into the abyss and said, "I just can't face it." To add to their misery, those managers who went ahead were met by a blocking, unhelpful human resources department that was extremely reluctant to advise the manager or support them with attendance at an internal hearing. They were entirely and openly sympathetic to any employee facing dismissal, whatever the circumstance. As one boss told me, "I'm not a coward, but when you're sitting on your own on one side of the table, and they've got a union rep, a friend, and someone from HR sitting with them, glaring at you, it's daunting." Weak and unprofessional HR staff can be a very real hindrance to tackling problems that should be resolved.

These terribly difficult people can cause us to worry, fester and exaggerate the possibilities. An old Swedish proverb says that "worry often gives a small thing a big shadow" and that is exactly what happens with these mythically untouchable employees. They cast a big shadow and they know it. But none of that solves the problem. As time ticks on, more damage is done, you look weaker as a manager, morale heads downhill and you gradually devalue good contributions by continuing to fund and accept the substandard ones. Better to put the fears aside. Confront the problem.

Armageddon is unlikely. Things move on remarkably quickly. We work within a contract. There are two parties to it.

When people are made redundant or laid off

Strictly, a job or position is redundant and not a person. True redundancy should mean you, as an employer, are no longer in need of that kind of work at all, or don't need as many people to perform the work. Genuine reasons for redundancies would include closing the business, closing down a workplace, or having a decreasing need for the employee's particular work skills.

But you may have noticed something odd happening in a lot of businesses and large companies. People are made redundant when that work clearly is continuing at a steady pace and the business is doing fine. So many people in the 80s and 90s and beyond faced redundancy that it has become a commonplace sight on a lot of resumes.

It can be viewed as a windfall for those who felt the need of a change or those who are confident they'll find other work without too much trouble. Sometimes people use their payment to take a break or a holiday or start something they've wanted to do for a long time. Managers are also offering redundancy packages as an easier way of shedding poor performers.

That can appear to be a "win-win" situation since the employee can say they were made redundant rather than dismissed for not doing their job – it looks better on a CV. Who complains about taking a payment package to leave if the alternative was to be dismissed? The risk is that the manager may have set a precedent for rewarding poor performance with a large payment.

Redundancy "rights" usually only become payable after a period of continuous service. Payments also depend on the employee's age, their complete years of service, their existing salary, and any extra acts of generosity the employer cares to make. There is a distinction between voluntary and involuntary redundancy, and in some large organizations there are often real opportunities to find alternative work for people.

"Laid off" is also a term that is often misused. Technically, it refers to work that has dried up but is expected to come back. In theory, the employee could be needed back in future. In other words, you don't have the work for people now but you expect this situation to be temporary. There are pockets of industries and business where people get used to the peaks and troughs and know that the call to stay home is a temporary thing.

However, you might have also noticed that the phrase "laid off" is often applied to cutbacks that are of a more permanent nature. When used correctly, lay-offs are understood and the rights of those affected are covered by agreements of fairly long standing. Some agreements mean that people are paid even though they have no work to do.

Remember, if this is a genuine redundancy or lay-off or cutback, then this person is leaving through no fault of their own. So redundancies, lay-offs and cutbacks require a different conversation to a disciplinary or dismissal situation.

You can still mark the departure of someone who is made redundant with a simple gathering and some recognition of their contribution. This is especially important if the person has been with you for some time. Don't go on about how wonderful they are because it will grate on their nerves and they may understandably ask "if I'm so wonderful, how come you're letting me go?"

Being made redundant or losing work through cutbacks need not be a terrible shock when employees are kept informed of the state of the business. With honest information, many will have thought through the worst-case scenario and faced the possibilities. Some may even volunteer for redundancy if it meshes with other decisions they are making.

But don't assume that everyone will be calm and relaxed about the news. Some may be in shock when they hear it, and you can never underestimate the value people place on their work and the pride they get from it. This might seem to be an out-of-date notion – particularly to a cynic or someone who doesn't care for their own work – but for many people, work is still a primary source of self-esteem and a place where they feel a sense of achievement, have steady companionship and a structure to their day. Losing employment through no fault of their own can carry the emotional impact of a divorce.

If you have to let people go because of a downturn then consider whether there's anything you can do to help. Small things might be greatly appreciated, such as allowing time off to apply for other jobs, or giving access to IT equipment to search job sites or write resumes and applications. Can you help them write a resume? It's not unheard of for businesses to appeal to their competitors to take on staff. Can you help employees to find the next job? It makes good business sense and it's a decent thing to do.

Employees might even be able to help the business. Maybe they can do more to find new customers. In some businesses employees have agreed to pay freezes and other measures to help keep the workplace going.

Security

In less organized workplaces, the announcement of sudden cutbacks, insolvencies and receivership management can signal the start of looting. Accountants can be seen arriving with new locks and keys.

You do need to be very aware of the potential for theft in hard times, especially if there are rumors of bankruptcy in the air. This is not to suggest that everyone is a thief – but be aware that this can happen. You need swift and careful management to prevent loss at these times.

Theft (whether redundancies are announced or not) is still gross misconduct. I recall a supervisor who encouraged her team to take anything that wasn't bolted down as her office faced closure. She freely abused sick leave in the months before leaving, claiming she was entitled, as if she wasn't being paid. She was not only being paid, she was looking at a generous redundancy package. This was the standard she chose to set as the manager.

How and where to cut back if you possibly can

Victor Kiam, who once famously purchased Remington and said about his shaver, "I liked it so much, I bought the company," was asked in an interview how he turned around a famous brand name product from near bankruptcy. "When your business is in a life raft," he said, "you have to get rid of the people who aren't rowing."

Who is going to help this business survive and grow? Alternatively, who is dragging it down or making success more difficult? You may not be the owner or even a part owner in the business. If so, I suggest you do the same as was advised in the chapter on Finding People – pretend it's your own money.

Cuts should always be made from the top first. When employees see that management have made reductions at their own level and frozen luxuries, perks, management raises and bonuses, the news of more cutbacks is understandably received a little better.

Forget what happened ten years ago. What are people doing today? What does merit look like right now?

To borrow from management consultant and academic, Michael Le Bouef, reward:

- Those who give you solid solutions rather than quick fixes.
- Those who take risks rather than those who avoid them.
- Those who are creative rather than those who always conform.
- Those who prefer to take action rather than endlessly analyze.
- People who work smart rather than hard.
- People who come up with simplifications rather than complications.
- Those who are quietly effective rather than those who make a lot of noise and produce very little.
- Those who produce quality when it's asked for.
- Those who are genuinely loyal.

- Those who can work with others rather than those who prefer to compete too much.

In short, hang on to the productive talent and lose the deadwood. Take the opportunity to help your business survive and prosper and say goodbye to poor performers, even if one of them is your Uncle Bert.

CHAPTER EIGHT

MANAGING TEAMS, CONFLICT AND CHANGE

HOW COULD TEAMWORK BE A PROBLEM?
WHAT IS GOOD TEAMWORK?
TALKING TO THE TEAM: Meetings, Briefings and Toolbox Talks
TEAM BUILDING FOR HUMAN BEINGS
MANAGING A CONFLICT WITHIN A TEAM
MANAGING CHANGE

*

> *A team of champions will never beat a champion team.*
>
> > Unknown

> *A committee is a cul de sac down which ideas are lured and quietly strangled.*
>
> > *Sir Barnett Cocks, British politician*

Teams are capable of producing fantastic results. A group of individuals working together can produce something that is far greater than they would on their own. There can be great personal satisfaction gained from being part of a good team.

Teams can also be destructive. Members can cancel out each other's talents. They can behave like lemmings and enthusiastically take a business over a cliff.

This chapter is about fostering the former and trying to avoid the latter in the workplace. A competent boss needs some extra skills in order to do this, such as good briefing skills and conflict management. Since change is the only constant in our working lives, a decent boss also needs to understand how to bring in changes with minimal disruption.

HOW COULD TEAMWORK BE A PROBLEM?

Teams can be problematic and go off on tangents for many reasons.

First of all, consider relationship dynamics. William James, American philosopher and psychologist, explained it well; "Whenever two people meet there are really six people present. There is each man as he sees himself, each man as the other person sees him and each man as he really is."

Now make that a team of five people and start to calculate how many relationships are really present. Make it a team of twelve and add up the pairings, trios, cliques and subgroups. There are a lot of relationships going on in any one team. Think about all the potential for people to have destructive conflicts, grating communications, or to simply go off into the wilderness together, reinforcing each other's poor sense of direction.

Secondly, there is the risk of "groupthink." This is a term coined by psychologist Irving Janis to describe a pressure that holds people back from speaking openly and consulting their own experience, wisdom and intelligence in the face of a powerful group. Smart, independent and responsible people have shown themselves to be very capable of stifling their own judgment and going along with the group's will or decision. People may worry about losing the tag of "team player" because they want to question the group's decision. The "let's stick together" speech can be directed at the individual who has real concerns. It can be an effective way of keeping people in line.

You can spot the stifling effects of groupthink on our freedom to speak after some meetings. People gather in corridors or call each other to quietly discuss their real opinions on issues. Genuine argument and debate can be saved for toilets, coffee talk, lunch tables or bars. There are very real dangers to a business and to the public when people who work together focus too much on being united in their thinking.

Why is the group so powerful? The answers lie partly in our basic needs to connect with other human beings and our desire to be liked and loved. Experts on human behavior, such as Stanley Milgram, Solomon Asch, Philip Zimbardo and Irving Janis, have demonstrated – sometimes with rather chilling experiments – just how dangerous the group can be and how an individual can put aside their own responsibility in the face of authority or peer pressure. You don't need an eminent psychologist to tell you this. Pick up a copy of today's paper and you're bound to find an example of the grim consequences of an individual following a mob and failing to use their own good sense. Or watch the superb Alec

Gibney documentary on Enron's demise, *Enron: The Smartest Guys in the Room* and consider whether teamwork is always worth cultivating.

A third problem with teamwork, and it's linked to the second problem of not thinking for ourselves, is our sense of responsibility when we're in a group. There is an old adage: one boy is a boy, two boys is half a boy and three boys is no boy at all.

To illustrate this point in an example that is far from the typical working day, consider the tragic case of Kitty Genovese, who bled to death on the pavement of a New York street in 1964. Thirty-eight people had heard or witnessed three separate attacks on Kitty. No one went to her assistance or called the police.

> The lesson is not that no one called despite the fact that thirty-eight people heard (Kitty's) scream, it's that no one called *because* thirty-eight people heard her scream. When people are in a group ... responsibility for acting is diffused. They assume that someone else will make the call, or they assume that because no one else is acting, the apparent problem ... isn't really a problem.
>
> Malcolm Gladwell, *The Tipping Point*

Don't imagine that this is a story about New York and its citizens' peculiar indifference. This story happens throughout the world. I lived in Hong Kong for a time and recall the news story of an elderly Chinese woman who died slowly on a pavement beside a busy newspaper stand. Her ordeal lasted through the morning rush hour. The newspaper seller ignored her cries for hours and thousands of people walked past her. Most would have carried mobile phones and pagers of some kind. Not one person intervened or even made an anonymous call for help.

It appears that we're more likely to act or get involved if we're alone. If we see someone fall over on the pavement and we're the only person around, we might be more inclined to rush to their aid. If it happens in a crowded place we might assume someone else will do something.

The lesson for bosses from these grim tales is that it's more likely that employees will turn away from a real problem, hoping that someone else will do something when they're part of a large group. Responsibility is diluted in teams.

When the employee who does speak up about a problem is alienated, punished, labeled a whistle-blower or kicked out of a job, there's an added incentive to stay quiet.

A fourth problem with teamwork is that human beings are still self-centered creatures. We still have a need for individual rewards and attention. Most human beings still ask the question "What's in it for me?" We may also prefer to work alone and collect praise for our singular achievements.

And a fifth big sticking point is that happy teams may not be all that productive anyway. Even the slightly dysfunctional team may produce great work. People may work well together, but it doesn't mean the end result will be a good one. Some creative partnerships, for example, have been known to produce brilliant work even when the two parties can barely tolerate each other.

Some teams probably work well because they rarely meet. They may be located across time zones, on different kinds of contracts (part-time, freelance, remote work, subcontract) and a manager may struggle to get everyone together in one room.

It's not easy to sustain a high performing team even if the names stay the same. Think about how many successful music groups stay together and continue to perform and create successfully as a team. It's fairly common to find acrimonious splits instead.

Some teams are hard to be around and may impact turnover. In melodramatic teams the mood can be too manic. Every day is described as a nightmare, and terms like "fighting fires" are over-used. This is hard going on the more stoic and even-tempered employees. Melodramatic teams are often led by bosses who believe that busy equals good. The behavior is modeled and reinforced. The panic merchants become the favored children. The leader might tell you that "we work hard and we play hard." Usually they don't do either. They don't work smart and the play is sometimes a case study in arrested development.

Teams where politics, games and one-upmanship are palpable are also hard to cope with for the quiet achievers. They can also be ineffective because time and energy is diverted away from the result required. The customer is often short-changed by this kind of working atmosphere.

Silos or tribes can focus inward so much that they stop sharing information, limit their interactions with others, and start obstructing other teams. They start competing or seeing themselves as an entirely separate and more valued group. They may reject the wider organization, particularly when the whole business needs to change. This becomes abundantly apparent when the silo protests loudly that they should be exempt from the changes or rules because "we do things differently in our group."

A mistake many bosses make in recruiting is that they try to find people who fit in to the existing team. The smart move is to find people who bring in differences, particularly the kinds of skills and experiences you're lacking. The easiest way to achieve groupthink is to keep recruiting the same kinds of characters and subtly punish people for thinking differently.

So teams can be a problem, and a boss needs to avoid fostering a team that is:

- working against itself.
- wasting time, money and effort on politics, sabotage and destructive in-fighting.
- burying problems or ignoring them.
- heading off in a direction that is away from the plan.
- causing problems to the rest of the business and the customers.

WHAT IS GOOD TEAMWORK?

How do you shape a good team? The lessons about shaping behavior in individuals remain the same. Leading teams still demands the same awareness of modeling and reinforcement. What you do and say is critical. What you reward, ignore or criticize will still be the biggest influence on a team's behavior.

If you praise people for sharing information and supporting others in the team, then you'll probably see better teamwork all around. If everyone can see that you value and favor the prima donna who will not cooperate, then you'll inevitably get the opposite.

Leaders still need to manage individuals within the team. Employees are not hidden by a team, and leaders should not abdicate their responsibility for performance management to the team. For example, a good boss would never criticize the whole team when they really need to talk to one person. You can't leave the group to sort out the person who is falling under par. This is abdication, and basic cowardice, but most of all it is ineffective and will diminish you in the eyes of the entire team. The person needing to take in the necessary feedback won't hear it because it's not aimed at them. The people who did not deserve the criticism will understandably feel cheesed off.

Conversely, imagine hearing the group being praised for something you did alone? What a slap in the face it would be if other team members did nothing to contribute, or even hampered your efforts in some way.

Having everyone in agreement all the time does not mean good teamwork exists. If people nod and agree with everything you say then you need to check their drinks. People see things differently. Their perceptions and opinions are changeable and unique, making it almost impossible or rare to get absolute agreement. Consider how many people will read today's paper and the likelihood of two people forming exactly the same opinions over the headline stories. Consensus is about freely admitting "I don't agree but I can live with that."

Good teamwork is not necessarily about happy smiling people singing "Kumbaya" either. Once again, drinks may need to be checked. Indeed, highly successful work teams may have a healthy level of tension and competition. You're aiming for people to cooperate to get the job done, to share information and support each other. If they get along then that's a bonus.

You can find a lot of material on the factors that make a good team. You can even think back to good teams you've been a part of and come up with your own list. Just be aware that good teamwork in the workplace is different to a football team. Some principles will be similar but the workplace is not a football field.

In good teams, members help each other to learn and adapt to changes quickly.

Good teams draw strength from a shared goal, a habit of mutual support and their collective history.

One enduring source of good sense in the subject comes from Mike Woodcock and John E. Jones who suggested there were nine factors present in effective teams.

- Clear objectives and agreed goals
- Openness and confrontation
- Support and trust
- Cooperation and constructive conflict
- Sound procedures
- Appropriate leadership
- A regular review of their teamwork
- Individual development
- Sound intergroup relationships

You might notice that the key management functions of planning, leading, organizing and controlling dovetail very nicely into this list. For example, in the leader's support for planning, the team develops clear objectives and agreed goals. In organizing, they develop sound procedures. Their regular review sets up a control function so that the team can check how it's doing against the plan.

Leadership in good teams is at an appropriate level. It's an interesting word – appropriate. It requires you to consider how "hands on" you need to be. What style of leadership is right for this team? Your overall aim is to encourage independence, not anarchy. A useful first step is to consider what is needed in terms of your leadership style. "If it ain't broke, don't fix it" might just work. Don't impose heavy interference if a team is functioning and only requires continued support.

Working life is changing and so are work teams. Teams are not static entities. Even if you kept exactly the same people and their work barely changed, their needs and wants would change over time. The customers would be changing. With flattening hierarchies and less rigid ideas about rank and formality, some teams may even rotate the role of leader.

Even if you inherit a very demoralized team, keep in mind that the atmosphere can turn around very quickly. If you want to improve teamwork and people believe you're being honest then you can count on a few allies who also want a better working day, because people generally like to connect and belong to something that's positive and enjoyable.

Some useful review questions for any team

Using the Woodcock and Jones factors as a base, the following questions can be a gauge to check how any team is doing. You could hand these questions to a neutral observer, or ask the team to rate themselves and talk about the good, the bad and the ugly. Of course, it's not always easy to start an honest conversation about a problem. If a team ticks all these boxes quickly and claims "no problem here" you can guarantee that the opposite is true.

- Does everyone understand the purpose of the team, the overall plan, and how the team's plan fits into the business plan?
- Are people's actions consistent with achieving the goals of the team?

- Do people share concerns honestly or raise issues in a constructive manner?
- Do they attack the issue or the individual/s involved?
- Does the team avoid issues that are difficult or unpleasant?
- Do people listen to each other? If not, why not?
- Do people feel they are gaining something or improving in some way while they're in this team?
- Is good use made of the time available when the team works together or meets?
- Does the team discussion focus on facts and objective information more than speculation, gossip and opinion? Is the balance out of kilter?
- When the team has a meeting, do actions come from the discussion?
- Does this team have good relationships with other groups and customers? Have they become a silo? Do they say things like, "We stick together! It's us against them." This can masquerade as good teamwork but it's not necessarily and it may backfire. And if the group doesn't share information or cooperate with other groups they will suffer for it in the long run when those other groups get their own back.

Setting some ground rules

Good teams and good meetings often have a few ground rules in order to maintain control and focus. You don't need many but they ought to be clear and relevant. Half a dozen are manageable.

Some common ground rules:

- Don't get sidetracked.
- One person speaks at a time.

- Only raise an issue or argument if it's relevant.
- Argue the issue. Don't attack the person.
- No negative comments about those who are not present.
- Respect the skills and experience of everyone in the team.
- Respect the time or observe basic punctuality as a courtesy to others.
- Let someone finish what they're saying.
- Ask the question. The only dumb question is the one you didn't ask.
- Mobile phones should be turned off.
- Laptops are put away if they're not being used for the meeting's purposes.
- No side conversations.

You don't have to choose the ground rules. In fact it's a great idea to have the group choose their own ground rules. We're more likely to agree with rules when we've had a say in their creation, but it is important that you uphold them and that you're prepared to remind others to keep to them. If you don't observe the ground rules then why would anyone else?

TALKING TO THE TEAM: Meetings, Briefings and Toolbox Talks

Managers will invariably address people in groups. Three typical gatherings that you will organize as a boss will be meetings, team briefings, and toolbox talks.

Every gathering at work needs planning, leading, organizing and controlling so that the time is used effectively. One of the greatest wastes of resources is the wasting of people's time.

Planning: Plan to achieve an outcome.

- Decide whether this should be a meeting, briefing or toolbox talk.
- What is it supposed to achieve or what is being sought here – action, agreement, learning or some other objective?
- How much time is likely to be needed?

Leading: Run every meeting with a sense of purpose.

A good leader, or chair, also makes sure that everyone contributes through questions and encourages people to bring in their relevant facts and observations. A good leader or chair enforces the ground rules.

Organizing: Go back to your plan and consider what is needed to achieve it.

- What is the right time of day to hold this gathering?
- Does someone else need to contribute input of some kind?
- Has everyone been informed of the necessary details?
- What materials are needed? (Paper, equipment, refreshments?)
- What are you going to say?
- What will be handed out?
- If this is a meeting, have you allocated timings on your agenda?
- Have you cleared a location and the likely interruptions such as noise, phones and people walking through?

Controlling: Will the gathering meet its objective? How will you know that?

Meetings

Meetings require an agenda, however brief or basic. Meetings without an agenda are just conversations.

The worst meetings drag on because the chair isn't strong, the issues don't progress, and inaction is tolerated. There are other reasons for the time waste including gossip and heading off on tangents.

Question how much time is absolutely necessary. Historian C. Northcote Parkinson said that "Work expands to fill the time available for its completion." And so it is with meetings. Make a point of questioning any workplace gathering that has become so regular that people treat it as a fixed part of the business week. Gathering just to update each other on "what's happening" is wasted time. This can be done more effectively through other means. If you are very attached to it, at least make it snappy.

Meetings are held to generate discussion on actions required, but because everyone can speak at meetings, the problem of managing egos and manners arises. Deep-seated conflicts can also be noticeable when people gather. Frustrations are obvious too. It's noticeable when people have withdrawn and no longer bother to contribute. It's obvious when people are playing games or dominating the discussion for their own agenda. It's sadly too obvious when a meeting is ailing because it has descended into "who shouts loudest wins" or where people speak for the sake of speaking and don't add any value to the conversation. Let's be honest – meetings can be atrocious.

This is a good reason to create ground rules that help to manage a lot of the destructive behavior that can seep into a meeting room.

> *Search all the parks in all your cities. You'll*
> *find no statues of committees.*
> David Ogilvy, founder of Ogilvy and
> Mather advertising

Extremely extraverted people can adore meetings. One reason is that they get a spark of energy from being close to people. Extraverts tend to enjoy talking, thinking out loud, and being among a bit of action – or failing that, talking about action. This is a generalization.

Very introverted people can feel the opposite way. They tend to go to meetings with a slight sinking feeling and watch the clock, hoping it will be over soon. They'd much rather get on with their work, do not appreciate having to speak until they've thought something through, and find being around people – particularly loud people – a bit of a drain on their energy. This is another generalization.

And sadly there are those folk who feel that their personal worth is increased by the number of meetings they attend. They like to tell their nearest and dearest that they've been busy in meetings all day. They would rather say "I'm in a meeting" than honestly admit "I was having lunch." These folk can be the first to resist the idea of reducing or cutting meetings that don't add value.

You're not going to change these traits, but you can run meetings that are fit for purpose and pacify most tempers. You could allow people to consider an issue and come back later with opinions. You could hand out available information beforehand to be read. This will suit your introverts and should improve the standard of contributions.

In spite of all the negative comments above, there are still very good reasons to hold meetings.

Emails and calls can help to progress an issue, but meetings can be a very fast way to share useful information and collectively solve a problem. They are good for discussing opportunities and ideas, if they're well managed. The team gets away from the task and has a chance for a helicopter view of the situation. Team members can bring in information that others need to know. Meetings can boost productivity if the best ideas can come forward and be acted upon. Team members can learn from each other, and meetings help to build supportive relationships. There can be great humor and a sense of fun in a lot of meetings.

But the first question is always – must there be a meeting? And the second question is – if we don't have this meeting, will we still achieve the result we're aiming for?

Some other tips for running better meetings:

- Meetings should have invited attendees and an agenda.
- Start on time. If you wait for people, you're punishing those who were on time and rewarding latecomers. Guess what will start happening?
- Make sure everyone is clear about why the meeting is necessary.
- Stick to the agenda.
- Encourage people to speak without going on forever. Let people finish as long as it's relevant. Politely shut down anything that is not to the point.

- Observe your ground rules.
- Call on people to contribute if the meeting is dominated by a few.
- Ensure the meeting generates actions.
- Do not put "Any Other Business" on your agenda. Why? Because you might as well write "invitation to waffle." If someone raises an important issue that could not possibly have been put on the agenda in time, then deal with it, but don't get into the habit of allowing the meeting to be hijacked by late additions.

If you can, hold meetings toward the end of the day with reasonable time to get through the business by day's end. In this way everyone attending will have a vested interest in moving it along and going home on time – except for those who don't want to go home. Another tip is to plan it in a reasonable timeframe leading up to lunch and people will also want to move things along so they can eat.

Briefings

Team briefings are great for keeping people informed about what's going on and if there are any changes that will affect their work or well-being. They are a good way to manage time and costs by giving everyone relevant and useful information at once. In some workplaces, a team briefing starts or closes every shift or working week.

It's very common to hear employees complain that they're not told what's going on. It is also common to hear supervisors and managers complain that they try to tell people what's happening, but they're just not interested, or that "they only want to know about their pay."

You might think it's not easy to interest short-term temps, casual labor or negative employees, but press on. Run your briefings to appeal to your more positive employees and those who are interested in the business.

You have to imagine you are one of the team when you prepare for the briefing. How does this impact on them?

Team briefings tend to be a little one-sided. Their role is to impart information, so they're mostly one-way with questions held until the end.

- Keep it short and sweet. There's a reason why it's called a briefing. Twenty minutes is plenty of time. People might be standing, and most of us have a limit in how much listening we can do in one burst.
- Try to make it relevant and interesting.
- Inject enthusiasm if appropriate – even if it's a very routine task.
- Make sure there is some opportunity to ask questions.
- Leave the group knowing where to go for further information.
- Always get back to people if they raise a concern.
- If there's anything of particular concern to one person, then tell them you'll talk it through with them at the end. Don't keep everyone else waiting. This is especially important when others are standing.

Toolbox Talks

Toolbox talks are generally quick, portable training sessions. Sometimes they occur in lunch breaks and have some name that references the fact that it's OK to listen while you eat.

Most bosses and subject matter experts will give these and they are usually delivered on site. They should only hit one topic at a time, which can suit health and safety subjects, the use of equipment, a demonstration of a new product or line, the explanation of a minor change to a work method or procedure, or any short training topic relevant to your business.

Some tips for making training and toolbox talks more effective:

- Make sure there is one key learning point.
- Keep it under twenty minutes.
- Try to get the training across in a mixture of ways – don't just lecture.
- Try to get those standing about to do something with the new learning. That can be as simple as having a quick quiz or asking for experiences. Any training is enhanced when the learner is able to try out the new skill or knowledge.
- Allow questions as you go along.

Please don't try to break a major training program into twenty-minute lunchtime slots. You cannot impart all types of training effectively through toolbox talks.

TEAM BUILDING FOR HUMAN BEINGS

Once upon a time, companies with more money than sense put on crazy team-building events and called them training. These often encompassed activities that coerced normally sane people to abseil, climb walls, fall backwards from a height and trust colleagues to catch them, swim through spider-infested caves, get lost in jungles or walk across hot coals chanting "Yes! Yes! Yes!" The day would generally end with a group hug.

I wish I was kidding.

Early in my career I had to supervise a five-day circus that turned sixty mild-mannered service employees into slogan chanting, over-tired fanatics. Had the lead trainer, I'll call him Robbie, suggested to some participants they should run naked through the streets I'm sure they would have complied. Groupthink was very obvious at these events, and individuals routinely went against their better judgment to be swept along by the team. A tourist wandering by asked me if we were teaching employees to be obedient. Robbie was terrifyingly reckless and I spent five days fearing a serious accident because of his obvious lack of responsibility.

If you have failed to send your team through one of these experiences then you have done them a great kindness, saved money for more worthwhile purposes, and avoided one of the greatest embarrassments of corporate training.

Thanks to the stronger duty of care placed on managers in many countries, these things are dying out but they have not entirely gone away. As I was writing this chapter, a colleague told me that her daughter was pressured into joining in a laser skirmish night as part of a team-building event. Robbie is still touting for team-building business in his part of the world.

It's not acceptable to risk injury in the name of team-building when we are rightly trying to achieve a zero tolerance attitude to accidents in our working day. What message does it send to talk about safety and then tell people that it is character-building to walk across hot coals?

Good team-building should never simulate or risk distress, injury or hysteria. Pushing people to the point of exhaustion and tears is not adult learning.

We might ask these questions before we set up any team-building task:

- What are the consequences for those who fail?
- What happens to those who show rational fear and distress?
- What happens when they have to come into work on Monday and carry on as normal?
- What happens to the claustrophobic or the employee with vertigo who is pressured for possible promotion to undertake some activity that pushes them too far?
- What right does an employer have to subject employees to something so irrelevant to the work they are paid to do?

Businesses that reward good teamwork and a great result with some social gathering or trip somewhere are not doing any harm, but again, there must be choices and people should not feel uncomfortable if they don't wish to participate. This sounds so obvious but a colleague was once ridiculed because she didn't want to sit through a strip show. She was attending a weekend away with the otherwise male management team to discuss strategy.

Sports and games can be great fun if people are genuinely having a good time and have a choice, but any sport chosen will not be fun for those who can't play, burn easily, lack co-ordination, don't care, or still have nightmares about being forced to play sport at school. Even a drinks gathering, and I love to go out for drinks, can be difficult for people who do not drink, are trying to give up drinking, losing weight or perhaps feel sick around the smell of alcohol. I know this all sounds a bit harsh, but the point is to give people some choices and put some thought into anything that is outside of an employee's contractual obligations at work.

It may sound as though I'm suggesting that all team-building efforts are nonsense, but that's not the case and I'd be a hypocrite to suggest this when I have run plenty of them. There are responsible and thoughtful team events that have some "fun with a purpose" but they are focused and stay on an adult level. There can be great value in taking people out of the workplace from time to time. Teams just forming can benefit from getting to know each other in a relaxed setting. Taking time out to work through information-sharing issues or gain clarity of roles can be very useful. It's also good to talk about what the team does well, so that you don't lose those qualities.

Successful "away days" or team-building events have a clear purpose. If the purpose is getting to know each other, then focus on that. They require the same planning, leading, organizing and controlling as other gatherings but in addition to this, a good boss will think it through and apply some sensitivity and common sense. This is what managers are paid to do anyway.

MANAGING A CONFLICT WITHIN A TEAM

Conflict is a normal part of the working day. People see things differently. They approach tasks in different ways. There is always a conflict over resources. And if we think of the word "conflict" as simply meaning "a difference" then we can accept that it must be inevitable and add it to the list of things which must be managed.

A constructive conflict is where bad feelings are at a minimum. Parties don't take things personally because attention is focused on solving the problem, not on the individuals. The mutually shared goal is improvement. Team members seek a win-win resolution. A level of constructive conflict exists in high functioning teams that have ground rules.

In destructive conflicts, the parties can engage in lose-lose behavior. Negative feelings dominate. There may be little interest in the other side's point of view or needs. There may be little interest in resolving the conflict. A destructive conflict in the team you manage can ignite feelings of fear, insecurity and anxiety for all those affected.

Peter Drucker felt that conflicts tended to "arise from the fact that people do not know what other people are doing and how they do their work, or what contribution the other people are concentrating on and what results they expect. And the reason they don't know is that they have not asked and therefore have not been told."

Must you act at all?

Two extreme responses to a destructive conflict at work are rushing in and trying to fix it quickly, or hiding from it in the vain hope that it will resolve itself.

Those who rush in and want a quick solution may find they make matters worse. On the surface it may look like the problem is solved, but deep down the real causes of the conflict may still be there.

Those who prefer to avoid conflict may find they are neglecting their role as a leader and harming the workplace by their reticence.

It's important to restate that people who work together do not have to like each other. But team members *do* have to be able to work together and when a dispute affects the flow of work, disrupts the work of others, or damages the business then you need to do something about it.

You are, as ever, obliged to stop and think it through before rushing in and making the situation worse.

The focus of your discussion with the parties is about the future.

First of all, be very clear in your own mind, how is the work being affected and what needs to change?

Then determine what kind of conflict is going on. Is the conflict over resources, values and opinions or has it become emotional? Any kind of conflict can become emotional. They rarely start out that way.

If it's a significant ongoing conflict over resources such as machinery, money, time or labor, then do everything you can to sort it out. Help the parties come to an agreement or get the extra resource. The allocation of resources is your ultimate responsibility.

Is this a conflict of values or opinions? Perhaps the way work is carried out, the way customers are dealt with, the direction the business is taking, or the interpretation of policy or overall strategy is unclear. Can the two different values co-exist? Often they can. Is there a policy or guideline that resolves this? Is there some clarity you can provide, or find elsewhere?

Has it become emotional? Have anger and distress taken over? Is silence and stonewalling prevailing? As a manager, ask for an agreement to work together. If they won't sit in the same room then have that conversation twice. Some of the hardest conflicts to mediate are the personal and emotional. In situations like this, just state that you don't need to know all the background. You simply want to find a way for the parties to work together. Is there some way of avoiding or reducing the antagonism between them? Can they be physically separated so they don't need to see each other so much? Your aim is to get a solution that allows work to flow again, or the people around this conflict to feel able to work. Your aim is not to make the two parties into friends. Encourage people to try to disagree without being disagreeable. Telling people they are being silly or locking them both in an office until they sort it out could demean and infuriate one or both parties.

Is the behavior of one party clearly unacceptable? Is one refusing to compromise in any way? Has one party clearly broken an established practice, ground rule, or business guideline? Is it, in fact, a disciplinary issue?

Should this conflict be taken out of the workplace? I've witnessed some fairly unpleasant spats over religion, divorces, family problems and political views that disrupted work and should never have come into the workplace. And the same goes for the trivial. Arguments over football finals or who should be voted out of the latest reality TV show should really be saved for the lunch table. If you can hear it, then customers can probably hear it too, and it's likely to be disrupting other people trying to work.

If one party (or both) is not doing their work, or they are failing to follow reasonable instructions, then you have a disciplinary situation. The conflict is not an acceptable excuse. The message must be clear that the standards apply to everyone. A business still needs controls and you have every right to manage standards and controls.

Popular advice warns us never to take a side, but there are situations when you might side with right over wrong if one person is clearly in the wrong. You should always side with any agreement that has been made.

You may even ask both involved to consider if they would be better off elsewhere. Ask only one and you have clearly taken a side, which is fine if you clearly value one and not the other. You may feel justified in doing that, but get some legal advice before making the suggestion.

Try to remain as approachable, calm and objective as possible. For any major conflict you can call in a third party – a mediator or consultant that you trust – but don't abdicate all responsibility or involvement.

Don't ever expect a conflict to be all solved in a day. Sudden reconciliations, light-dawning epiphanies and crowd-cheering moments only happen in the movies. It will take some time to get things on an even keel.

MANAGING CHANGE

> *Change is caused by consultants. Then you need consultants to tell you how to handle the change. When you're done changing you need consultants to tell you that the environment has changed and you'd better change it again. It's a neat little perpetual motion machine. That's the problem when you pay consultants by the hour. In some small towns there is a rule that consultants can't serve as volunteer firemen. The fear is that they'd drive around setting fire to the town.*
>
> *Scott Adams, creator of* Dilbert.

Any working life is going to be full of risk and constant change. Standing still or resisting change will risk boredom, inertia, and eventual failure when we do not adapt to the changing world around us.

Resisting change is not just an issue for individuals. Giant corporations have fallen over because they did not see the need to change and became too comfortable with the status quo, too convinced that they would always be successful. Science warns us to adapt or die. The businesses that survive are inevitably the great adaptors.

Luckily most employees are also great adaptors. If you consider the many changes that have occurred in the average working life, you would have to conclude that people might not seem to love change but are quite resilient about it all the same.

The management of change, like a lot of other issues in this book, could easily fill a weighty manual on its own, and it often does. Change management is a fairly standard offering now in many management programs and degrees, but how you manage change is a major test of your patience more than anything else.

Do people always resist change? I believe the answer is – it depends. It depends whether they've had a say in it, whether they've had some warning about it, how they feel right now about their work, how many other changes are going on in their lives, whether they see something good in the change for themselves and whether they're inclined to trust the person introducing the change. So much depends on whether we understand why it's happening or why it's necessary.

The problem is not that human beings hate to change, it's that they dislike loss and try to prevent it from happening. Change represents a loss. To embrace change we have to give up on the way things are, and we need a good reason for doing that.

We are creatures of habit, fond of structures and consistency. If you've ever worked in a job with an employee car park, you may have noticed that people park in the same spaces every day and can get annoyed if someone is in their space. You might also notice that people tend to sit in the same area of the canteen and are similarly miffed if someone has taken their spot.

Some people will cling to bad habits, or even persist with something that isn't working rather than change to the unknown. Hence the expression, "Better the devil you know." At least that devil gives us a sense of consistency and feels predictable.

Don't underestimate the genuine pain and distress caused by a change. The small changes you think are so obviously needed, may incur enormous resistance. I've seen reactions to change that could easily be dismissed as foolish, unreasonable or even funny. But they successfully stalled necessary changes just the same.

And you can witness some curious behavior around change that isn't necessarily obstructive. One company began the process of changing its logo after being taken over. An employee asked if he could buy the company van he'd been driving for some years. It was assumed this was just another purchase of old fleet stock, possibly for one of his sons. In fact, he could not bear to see the sign changed on the side of the van and wished to keep driving it as it was. I watched a PA track down a printing firm that would provide her letterhead with the old company logo. She paid for the paper supply out of her own pocket. She was milking a directive to use up the old supply of paper first. A colleague told me about an employee who refused to upgrade to a new IT system and broke into the office at night to rewire his computer to the old mainframe.

Don't be surprised at the objects, tools, rules, traditions, work methods, systems, furniture layouts and rituals that people are attached to. If you have the chance, and you usually do, make the time to talk to people, listen to them and respect their right to feel the way they do. It's possible that some counseling would help. If the situation becomes impossible and drifts into a significant problem, then deal with it as you would any other performance matter.

And so change, like absolutely everything else you do as a manager, requires planning, leading, organizing and controlling. What's the plan, boss?

If you think that managing is simply about being decisive and tough, you might flinch at the idea of taking a bit more time with change, but this is where you need to slow down to go fast later on. If you crash through and forget that it is people who carry out change, then your effort will fail, or be remembered as something very painful for years to come.

You may think that everyone understands why the change is necessary. Think again. Be prepared to give honest information about what must happen and why. Talk about the risks of staying as you are. Do this until you're sick of it. Let me repeat that, because it's a big secret in the art of change management – give people as much information as possible, even if you have to repeat the same information until you're tired of it.

When you introduce a change, expect some people to pretend they haven't heard you, look puzzled, sabotage the change, or persist with the old ways. Some may even insist that your plan for change won't work, without giving it a proper try.

Respecting people's need to have a say doesn't have to drag on and hold up your plan, but steamrolling people causes problems. Welcome curiosity and questions. Think of the person asking the tough questions as a potential ally.

Good thinkers are an asset. Maybe the way they challenge needs some polish, but a tough question shows that they're thinking. It's the people who don't ask anything and don't attend any briefings that you might worry about.

Once the actual change has gone ahead, whether it's a merger or systems change or new uniform, then reinforce that change. Go back and ask people how they're going. Check to see if it's working and whether improvements are needed. Find out how people are coping, don't introduce a change and leave it. It will die.

Change comes with risks such as the possibility of feeling foolish or simply failing. Give people some time to try any change on for size.

Some other dos and don'ts for change

- Do consult with people as much as you reasonably can. Get the input of those affected. You might gather some important information that was missed.
- Break people into small groups to talk to them, and set up a test group from one of these if you can.
- Make sure people can easily get some coaching if they need it, or that they know who to ask for help. Make sure that appointed person is not hard to reach or difficult to talk to.
- Be positive and polite when people ask questions and want more information. It's so easy to feel your shoulders slump and wish you could say "Haven't we gone over this?"
- Try to stagger a big change if you can. If it can be broken into stages, do so. It's better for you to check against the plan and see that it's working.
- Don't expect to have instant acceptance on day one. That would be weird. It would go against human nature.

- Don't tolerate the begrudging resistance or sabotage for too long. Give people some rope, but not an endless right to scupper the change.

If you cannot express the benefit of a change in the clearest possible language then you will struggle to succeed with it. People will want to know why this is happening and how it will make things better. They will understandably wonder if the short-term pain is going to be worth it, and what is so terribly wrong with the way things are. If you can't answer the "why" question clearly, and if no one else can give you a straight answer, then why exactly are you doing it?

If you don't like the change, then you can say something like "Look I'm not a hundred percent sure about it either, but let's give it a genuine try and if we have a problem, let's talk about it." You can always show you can understand people's concerns without sympathizing with the saboteurs. If you work in a larger place that has introduced the change, find out all you can about the reasoning behind it. Never say something like "Well, here's another pea-brained idea from head office." You might think this – but now is the time to be a leader and a professional.

It's not possible to answer a question about the future with great confidence, since you can't see it, but here's where you find out if people trust you and think you know what you're doing.

Last of all, change management is not about sitting in a bunker with spreadsheets, diagrams and charts. I say this because many organizations today clearly think change is a process with logical solutions created on software programs. I saw this occurring in a large company introducing a new IT system. The change was disastrous, with costly overruns, angry staff, and the inevitable litigation. Planning is crucial, without question, but change is accepted and carried out by human beings.

Change management is about patience, talking, and active listening. It's about taking people from A to B – and that is entirely down to your ability to persuade and earn trust.

*

SOME CLOSING THOUGHTS ABOUT CHANGE AND DECENT MANAGERS

I recently had a work trip to a country in Asia that is now viewed as an economic powerhouse. That was not the case when I started work thirty years ago. In fact, one charity that benefited from our workplace donation scheme back in the 1980s was a nursing scholarship within this country. We clearly thought they needed our help. They clearly don't need it today.

This particular trip involved some large-scale safety meetings inside a very intensive manufacturing site. The managers I met were organized and focused. They treated everyone in the room as equals. They had worked hard to create a culture of safety within a highly profitable organization. Though their statistics were enviable, they understood the problem of complacency in safety. I thought about the rise of safety and the rise of this economy as I flew home. I started thinking about many things that had changed during my working life.

In my first real job for a large company some thirty plus years ago, it was something of a badge of honor to collect speeding tickets. I had several. I drove long distances, sometimes late at night, and it never occurred to me to manage those trips around the risk of fatigue. We had long alcohol-fueled lunches and a lot of "drinks after work." We drove home or staggered across busy roads after social events. Some of our fellow employees insisted that it was part of their job to get drunk with clients.

No one discussed this behavior as if it was a problem or a risk. There was an unspoken message – if you don't like it then go and work somewhere else. It was the culture, and – as is still true of many workplaces – people talked about culture as if it could never be changed.

Thirty years ago, getting senior managers into a room to talk about safety involved making them promises about food, alcohol, and a very short agenda. The meeting room, like all meeting rooms, would be filled with cigarette smoke by day's end. The safety guy in most places where I worked (and it was always a guy) was lucky if he was occupying a small office in the basement. His authority was dependent on the variable levels of courtesy granted by the management of the day. In one emergency drill, our most senior figure in the office refused to leave his desk and told the safety guy, "F*** off – I'm busy!"

Those attitudes are rare today. Things changed and suddenly it was not OK to be drunk at work, it was not OK to drink and drive, and it was not OK to yell expletives at the safety staff. Today, safety representatives in well-managed companies have a powerful voice and invariably sit at the top table.

The ethos of striving hard to ensure that nobody gets hurt still hasn't gone to every corner of industry (or the globe) but it has come a very long way. That is a great credit to the safety management profession and all the other managers who said "Enough! Let's change this." Their determination has meant that fewer people will die at work and fewer people will be maimed at work. Members of the public are safer, and arguably families and communities of those who caught the safety message have become safer.

This seems like an obvious aspiration today but it was a long haul for behavior change professionals. Some cultures shifted very slowly. Some are still in compliance mode.

There are other aspects of behavior – behavior that causes despair and worse, such as overt discrimination and bullying – that are now being addressed at least. I still see and hear my share of horror stories so I'm well aware there is work to be done but, on balance, I'm optimistic that the workplace is becoming a safer and more professional and humane place for my children's generation. And that has only happened because decent people wanted change and made it happen.

Unfortunately, there are other aspects of our working lives that appear to be going backwards.

If I am bewildered about something that has not improved, it is the glaring inequality in pay for women in Australia. It could change tomorrow but it just doesn't budge. In one company I worked for the gap stood at 34%, and the CEO said openly that he was comfortable with that. He was, at the same time, photographed handing over a sizeable sponsorship check for an aggressive male-dominated sport. The money might have gone to balancing the gender pay gap, but he wanted his place in the sponsor's box on game day and the shareholders still don't seem too concerned. There is no law in my country that can hold him to account for being comfortable with a 34% pay gap.

My fair-minded husband did not really believe that overt pay discrimination could possibly be happening in his own profession, while knowing it was common in the companies I had worked for. This changed when he heard of a married couple with equal qualifications and experience in financial accounting. A recruitment agent approached them separately about an opportunity. The agent did not realize the couple had married because the wife kept her surname. The starting salary offered to the husband was $40,000 higher than the amount quoted to the wife. The agency was well known and the calls were made on the same day. This happened in Sydney in 2014. The recruitment agent was female.

There has been constant attention paid to the issue of the gender pay gap in the media for the last few years. Not a week goes by without articles and speeches calling for action. But these calls from the exasperated and well-intentioned face a problem – they don't have the means to fix it. There are people working to correct this but there are too many managers who could act but clearly don't feel inclined to. Must we go to legislation, quotas, and punitive measures for managers who willfully, deliberately pay less to women for the same work? It appears so. Calls to the conscience are not working.

There are many other changes that I believe would give us more dignified workplaces. The profession of Human Resources needs a radical overhaul but I fear that won't happen while there are "People and Culture managers" (the new name for HR) who have their calls screened like royalty in case, heaven forbid, an employee or member of the public tries to speak to them. And would there be such a growing gap in gender pay if more HR people took an ethical stand and worked as hard as safety professionals did to say, "Enough! Let's fix this!"

E-recruitment systems need to be overhauled. Human beings should be coming back into the critical process of selecting people. The consultants who make money out of psychometric tests and know very well they are not going to give anyone definitive answers and are being misused and abused in the workplace need to take up some other line of work. There is plenty of work to do in the community for qualified psychologists.

While I'm dreaming, a note to photographers and business editors – can you stop the images of CEOs looking at us from the business pages with crossed arms and belligerent expressions? Can we have more work-related stories about the role models and bosses who are well-mannered and effective – according to their employees, and not according to a prize that the manager nominated themselves for? I recently witnessed a CEO help to create a leadership award for herself (yes, it's possible these days) while she was being counseled over bullying and poor self-control by her employer.

Wouldn't it be wonderful to see the big business schools run programs for leaders called How to Listen? Can we value the managers who aspire to being kind, approachable listeners rather than those who call themselves "transformational thought leaders?"

If some human beings lead lives of quiet desperation, can we strive to ensure it's not because they report to us on a daily basis? A bit more kindness, a bit more diligence and accountability and a bit less spin – this is what we need. Isn't this what we would like for our kids when they go to work and for what remains of our working lives?

Can we simply aim to do decent things? It is entirely possible to keep lifting the quality of life at work. Let's do what we can, when we can. Let me know how you're getting on and good luck.

ACKNOWLEDGEMENTS

A friend who kindly ran her eyes over a draft of this book said "I never realized you'd worked with so many awful people." Her comment stopped me in my tracks. Then I realized that I had gone to some dark corners of my memory for some examples. I apologize if these lean towards the negative end of the spectrum. This is not how I look back on thirty years of work either. I could count on one hand the former colleagues I'd cross the road to avoid. Of course there have been a few horror stories along the way, but we've all had those.

To set the record a little straighter I'd like to describe my first boss in my first year of work. I'm sure he viewed his primary role at work as a teacher and I learned a great deal as did many others who were fortunate to work for him. I only ever called him Mr. Smith and he only ever called me Miss Walmsley. He died some years ago but I often think how lucky I was to have such a well-mannered, gentle and steady human being as my first manager and mentor. I can still picture his slightly fatigued expression as I tried to justify my new theory of accounting, broadly called the "Near enough is good enough" method.

I have worked with some other fabulous managers besides Mr. Smith. They know who they are because I'm still in touch with them. Some have provided anecdotes for the book. Thank you to all of you.

On the subject of gratitude, I owe both Patricia Anderson and Anne Fussell a debt of many coffees for their keen observations and blue pencils. They made polite and gentle enquiries as to where I was hiding when grammar lessons were being held. I tried to reduce the jargon but I know it has crept in. I even removed the word "empower" from the draft when it caused Anne to break out in hives.

Sincere thanks also go to Colleen Bettridge and Suzie Dixon who read earlier chapters and versions of the book and the many colleagues and friends who continue to share their friendship and stories about the workplace with great humor. And thanks always go to Tony, my husband, partner and friend, whose counsel is always wise and whose support for this expensive hobby called writing is always steadfast.

This book recognizes all the people who were participants on hundreds of training programs, facilitated meetings and workshops that I ran over the course of my career. It is the pattern of their questions and repeated concerns in over thirty years that forms the structure of this book. Working in training, HR and the management of change allowed me to meet thousands of bosses who came from many different nationalities, professions, trades and corporate cultures. My work allowed me to travel the world and learn constantly. Most of all, it gave me the belief that most bosses are trying to do their best with what they know. I have rarely met a truly malicious boss. I've met a lot of very decent human beings and that has been a fortunate thing.

SOURCES OF QUOTES AND FURTHER REFERENCES

Introduction

Professor Henry Mintzberg (born 1939) is currently at McGill University in Montreal. *The Nature of Managerial Work* was published in 1973 by Harper and Row. He has been a key thinker on strategy and organizational structure. More recently Mintzberg published *Managers Not MBAs* (Mintzberg, 2004) and criticized elite business schools such as Harvard and Wharton for damaging the discipline of management by turning it into a science. He advocates greater emphasis in management education on action learning and extracting insights from real problems and experience.

Scott Adams (born 1957) is the cartoonist who gave us *Dilbert*. His quote "... me, I've gnawed an ankle or two" is from the introduction to *The Dilbert Principle* (Boxtree, 1996).

Charles Kuralt (1934–1997) was an award-winning American journalist. His full quote "The everyday kindness of the back roads makes up for the acts of greed in the headlines" comes from *On the Road*, first published in 1985 by Fawcett.

Chapter One

Mary Parker Follett (1868–1933) is considered to be one of the first management consultants. The quote comes from Metcalfe and Urwick's *Dynamic Administration: The Collected Papers of Mary Parker Follett* (Harper and Row, 1941).

Leonardo Da Vinci's quote: "You will never have a greater or lesser dominion than that over yourself ... the height of a man's success is gauged by his self-mastery, the depth of his failure by his self-abandonment ... And this law is the expression of eternal justice. He who cannot establish dominion over himself will have no dominion over others." Da Vinci was a painter, sculptor, architect, scientist, musician, mathematician, engineer, inventor, anatomist, geologist, astronomer, cartographer, botanist, historian and writer. He is widely considered to be one of the greatest painters of all time. Da Vinci was born in 1452 and died in 1519. This quote is from *The Notebooks of Leonardo da Vinci*, Richter (1888) XIX: The Philosophical, Maxims, Morals, Polemics and Speculations.

Cardinal Newman was born John Henry Newman in 1801. He died in 1890. His quote "Nothing would be done at all ..." comes from Lecture IX on *The Present position of Catholics in England* (1851).

Cicero (106–43 AD) was a Roman orator and politician and is credited for the quote "Only a fool persists in error ..." This can vary in its translation. Original Latin: *Cuiusvis est errare; nullius nisi insipientes, in errore perseverare.*

Chapter Two

Professor Barry Schwartz (born 1946) is an American psychologist who wrote *The Paradox of Choice: Why More is Less* (Harper Collins, 2009). Schwartz is currently Professor of Social Theory at Swarthmore College in the US.

Sue Townsend (1946–2014) was famously known as the creator of Adrian Mole. Her quote about the "avoidance of humiliation" comes from *The Sunday Times* (UK) 'Best of Times, Worst of Times' column in December 2002.

Andrew Cavendish (1920–2004) was the 11th Duke of Devonshire. The quote about his "terrible day" comes from an interview with Lyn Barber in *The Observer* (UK) in October 2002.

Chapter Three

Fran Lebowitz (born 1950) is a US journalist and humorist. The source of the quote "the opposite of talking ..." is from *Social Studies* (Random House, 1981).

Samuel Taylor Butler (1612–80) wrote the lines:
He that complies against his will
Is of his own Opinion still;
This is from the poem *Hudibras* and the complete stanza continues
Which he may adhere to, yet disown,
For Reasons to himself best known.

Ralph Waldo Emerson (1803–1882) was an American poet and essayist. The source of his "loaded eye can threaten" quote is from *The Conduct of Life* published in 1860.

Chapter Four

Premier Georges Clemenceau (1841–1929) was credited with a version of the saying "the cemeteries are full of indispensable men" by *Time Magazine* in November 1962, in an article titled "France, Close Victory." It is frequently misattributed to De Gaulle. Clemenceau was the Premier of France twice, from 1906–1909 and from 1917–1920. There is some dispute about the original source of this quote. It may have first come from an American publisher and writer Elbert Hubbard who wrote in 1907 "the graveyards are full of people the world could not do without." This was published in *The Philistine: A Periodical of Protest*.

E M Forster's (1879–1970) quote about spoon feeding was cited in *The Observer*, 1951 under "Sayings of the Week", but was recorded by the BBC in an interview with Forster in 1951.

Chapter Five

Clint Eastwood (born 1930) is an actor, producer, director and former politician. His quote comes from an interview where he was asked, "Do you think we're all in some way driven by inexplicable fate?" Eastwood replied, "Sometimes, yeah. I think sometimes certain things are just meant to happen for who knows what reason. I mean, I look back at myself at 15. I was a slow learner. Nowadays they have ADD and all these different syndromes, but when I was a kid we didn't have any of that. It was just, 'Mrs. Eastwood, your son is a little slow.' I'm striking a blow for C students everywhere. It took me a while to get my wheels rolling. I guess that's why they're still rolling at 74." This quote is from an interview with Richard Schikel for *Time Magazine* in February 2005, titled "How Lucky Does He Feel?"

Peter Drucker (1909–2005) was, as a writer and teacher, one of the greatest influences on modern management. He is quoted on the intrusion into personality from *Management: Tasks, Responsibilities, Practices* (Harper & Row 1973). Drucker was described by *Business Week* as "the man who invented management." The full quote from p.229 is "An employer has no business with a man's personality. Employment is a specific contract calling for a specific performance. Any attempt to go beyond that is usurpation. It is immoral as well as an illegal intrusion of privacy. It is abuse of power. An employee owes no 'loyalty,' he owes no 'love' and no 'attitudes' – he owes performance and nothing else ... The task is not to change personality, but to enable a person to achieve and to perform."

Chapter Six

Tom Peters (born 1942) is a writer on management and a renowned speaker on the subject of business and the workplace. The full quote is "Reject simple explanations. According to the press, I make my dough as a 'guru.' Revolting! That's not my take. I just talk about stuff I've seen, try to confuse people I talk to. Yet most who attend my seminars are looking for answers. Thanks for coming, but how tragic. There are no answers. Just, at best, a few guesses that might be worth a try." This quote comes from an article Peters wrote in the *Chicago Tribune*, December 1991, called "No Answers, just guesses that might be worth a try."

Pam Ayres was born in 1947. The full poem "The Battery Hen" is from *The Works: The Classic Collection* by Pam Ayres, published by BBC Books. Reprinted by permission of The Random Group Ltd.

Peter Drucker's quote "As we have known for a long time ..." is from the essay "How to make people decisions."

Barbara Ehrenreich (born 1941) is quoted from her book, *Nickel and Dimed: On (Not) getting by in America* (Henry Holt, 2001). Her later work, *Bait and Switch: The (futile) pursuit of the American dream* (Henry Holt, 2005) is a salutary observation on recruitment, coaching and outsourcing practices today.

Henry David Thoreau (1817–1862) was a US author, poet, philosopher and abolitionist. His quote "most men would feel insulted ..." is attributed to the essay "Life without Principle", first published in 1863.

Einstein's teacher's quote about being "adrift in his foolish dreams" can be found in *Asperger's Syndrome and High Achievement* by Ioan James (Kingsley Publishing, 2006) as a quote from Hans Einstein, the oldest son of Albert Einstein. Hans is quoted as saying that his father "told me that his teachers reported he was mentally slow, unsociable, and adrift forever in his foolish dreams."

Woody Allen (born 1935) is the writer and director of over fifty films. There are many versions of quotes about Woody Allen getting out of the way of the acting talent he hires. This particular quote came from an interview with US arts journalist Prairie Miller and took place on the *Arts Express* program for the National Radio Network in New York, February 2004, after the release of *Sweet and Lowdown*.

Clarence Francis (1888–1985) is credited with the quote "You can buy a man's time ..." Francis was a business executive and an internationally recognized expert on food production and distribution. Between 1940 and 1943 he assisted in defense mobilization for the US forces and was special consultant to President Eisenhower. This quote was first cited in the *Michigan Business Review* in May 1956 by DM Phelps in an article: "Starting the New Salesman Out Right."

Sir Michael Gambon was quoted in *The Telegraph* (UK), "Theatre's big bear is tied down at last" by John Whitley, 17 February, 2004.

Wentworth Dillon (1630–1685) was the 4th Earl of Roscommon. His quote "Immodest Words admit of no defense ..." is from his "Essay on Translated Verse" (1684).

George Bernard Shaw (1856–1950) was an Irish dramatist and winner of the Nobel Prize in Literature. The line "stupid man doing something he is ashamed of" is from his play *Caesar and Cleopatra*, first published in 1901 by Shaw in a collection, *Three Plays for Puritans*. This was later published by Penguin and is now in the public domain.

Chapter Seven

Steve Wright (born 1955) is a US comedian, actor and writer. He is also an Oscar-winning producer. The snake braiding story is from his 2007 album *I Still Have a Pony* from Comedy Central records.

Sir Peter Ustinov (1921–2004) was an Oscar-winning actor, dramatist, writer, raconteur and Ambassador for UNICEF, among many other things. He attended Westminster School in London and was reputed to have an early report that said "He shows great originality which must be curbed at all costs." This was cited in his obituary, March 29, 2004 in the *Sydney Morning Herald* (Australia).

Michael Le Boeuf (born 1942) is an American business writer and consultant and a former Professor of Management. His "Rules for reward" comes from *The Greatest Management Principle in the World* (Putnam Publishing Group, 1986).

Chapter Eight

The "team of champions" quote was first cited in an Australian newspaper, *The Adelaide Advertiser* in April 1911. It was then cited in October 1929 in *News*, also an Adelaide newspaper, and in May 1935 in the *Advertiser* again. There is no name attached to the sporting articles that contain this quote.

Sir Barnett Cocks (1907–1989) was a British politician. His quote "A committee is a cul de sac ..." is cited in Michael Moncur's *(Cynical) Quotations* and *Forbes Book of Quotations: 10,000 thoughts on the business of life*. It was first cited in *The New Scientist*, 1973.

William James (1842–1910) is sometimes referred to as the "Father of Modern Psychology." His quote "When two people meet ..." is from *Principles of Psychology*, first published in 1890.

Irving Janis (1918–1990) was a US psychologist and Yale professor. He coined the term "groupthink" in his book *Victims of Groupthink* (Houghton Mifflin, 1972). Groupthink occurs when a group makes faulty decisions because group pressures lead to a deterioration of "mental efficiency, reality testing, and moral judgment." Groups affected by groupthink ignore alternatives and tend to take irrational actions that dehumanize other groups. A group is especially vulnerable to groupthink when its members are similar in background, when the group is insulated from outside opinions, and when there are no clear rules for decision-making.

Milgram, Asch and Zimbardo are mentioned in the section on Teams and Groups. Dr. Stanley Milgram is known for the Milgram Experiments conducted at Yale in 1963. In 1973 he published *The Perils of Obedience* and in 1974 published *Obedience to Authority: an experimental view*. Dr. Solomon Asch is known for the Asch Experiments (also known as The Conformity Experiments) in the 1950s conducted at Swarthmore College. Dr. Philip Zimbardo is known for leading The Stanford Prison Experiment of 1971, sometimes referred to as the Prisoners and Guards experiment.

Enron: The Smartest Guys in the Room (Magnolia Pictures, 2005) was nominated for Best Documentary Feature at the 2006 Academy Awards. It was made by Alex Gibney who has since released *Going Clear: Scientology and the Prison of Belief*. This is also an excellent reference on group pressures and the problems with conformity.

Malcolm Gladwell (born 1963) is a journalist and author of *The Tipping Point: How Little Things Can Make a Big Difference* (Little Brown, 2000).

Mike Woodcock and John E Jones's work on effective teams can be found in, for example, *Woodcock's Team Development Manual* (Gower, 1985).

C. Northcote Parkinson (1909–1993) was the author of *Parkinson's Law* (1957). A scholar and naval historian, his quote about "work expanding so as to fill the time available for its completion" was first published in *The Economist* in 1955.

David Ogilvy CBE (1911–1999) was the co-founder of Ogilvy and Mather advertising. This quote about statues to committees is probably borrowed from a similar quote widely attributed to G K Chesterton (1874–1936). Ogilvy's phrasing comes from the article "David Ogilvy's best advice for Business?" by Patricia Sellers in *Fortune* magazine, July 21, 2009.

Scott Adam's quote about "change being caused by Consultants" is from *The Dilbert Principle* (Boxtree, 1996).

www.ingramcontent.com/pod-product-compliance
Lightning Source LLC
Chambersburg PA
CBHW030455210326
41597CB00013B/673